W9-CRR-999

CONTENTS

INTRODUCTION

This resource manual has been designed to assist instructors in using Samovar and Porter's *Intercultural Communication: A Reader,* Tenth Edition. This introduction includes suggestions for organizing the course, a brief description of chapter resources, and suggestions for leading post-exercise class discussions. In addition, instructional aids such as sample course schedules for both quarter and semester systems and a number of film, video, and internet resources are provided.

ORGANIZING THE COURSE

There are a number of ways to set up a college-level intercultural communication course. Some instructors use a culture-specific approach, where the communicative behavior of one or more specific cultures are studied. Other instructors follow a culture-general approach, where the influence of culture on the communication process is explored as it applies to nearly & cultures. There are also courses that emphasize specifically the psychological, sociological, or linguistic influences on intercultural communication. Some intercultural communication college courses are similar to intercultural training workshops because they emphasize experimental simulation and role-playing activities designed primarily to increase students' cultural sensitivity and intercultural communication competence. *Intercultural Communication: A Reader* provides a set of readings that would complement any one or combination of these approaches. The diversity of the articles provides instructors with enough flexibility to teach a course in intercultural communication based on their own personal teaching style and approach to the subject.

CHAPTER RESOURCES

Each chapter of this manual is divided into four sections: Chapter Synopsis, Discussion Questions, Exercises, and Test Items.

Chapter Synopsis

Each chapter synopsis provides a summary of each article included in the text chapter. Special points of interests are identified.

Discussion Questions

Many instructors prefer to incorporate class discussion as a primary mode of instruction. Therefore, each chapter offers discussion questions for each article that will inspire students to talk about the readings.

Test Items

Test items are included at the end of each chapter. Multiple choice, true/false and essay questions are provided for constructing examinations.

Exercises

Activities can be particularly engaging for students in an intercultural communication course. They offer a change from the traditional university lecture by allowing students to demonstrate and experience concepts provided by the instructor or the course textbooks. Additionally, using activities in the classroom is a powerful way to engage students in the course and in their own learning. Probably most important in the intercultural communication course is that activities transcend the classroom: "Instructional games, simulations, and role plays can enhance relevance of course material as students apply it in situations often designed to take them beyond the immediate classroom" (Nyquist & Wulff, 1990, p.350).

This manual offers a variety of instructional activities for each chapter of the text. The following is a description of each activity type and accompanying benefits.

Role-Play: Role-playing is a training activity where two participants (or more, though larger numbers are not common) take on characteristics of people other than themselves in order to attain a clearly defined objective. These "other people"—or roles—are usually fictitious, although they must be completely believable in the eyes of the training population for the role-play to work. Participants who are not actively involved in the role-play function as observers and look for certain things related to the overall objectives as the role-play unfolds (McCaffery, 1995, p. 19). Benefits include:

- Participants get a clear sense of identifiable skills in interpersonal situations, how they work, and the impact of things done effectively and ineffectively. -participants have an opportunity to feel what it is like to try out new or enhanced skills in real situations; and,
- Participants also get a chance to feel what it is like to be in another role. (McCaffery, 1995, p. 24)

Simulation Games: Simulation games provide interactive opportunities to practice new behaviors and experiment with new attitudes and points of view in a nonthreatening, nonjudgmental environment. They are particularly useful in intercultural training, since, in a very short time, they can stimulate cognitive and affective understanding and broaden participants' perspectives (Sisk, 1995, p. 82). Benefits include:

- Promotes critical thinking as participants analyze possible moves and probable consequences of those moves. Participants also must plan rationally and think through countermoves;
- Because chance is introduced, simulation games demonstrate that life is not always affected by logical plans or even intuitive solutions;
- Students learn on three levels: information, process, and strategies;
- Simulation games teach social values such as competition, cooperation, and empathy;
- Simulation games increase participants' knowledge and skills; and,
- Simulation games establish a sense of group dynamics and self awareness among participants. (Sisk, 1995, p. 89)

Critical Incidents: Critical incidents are brief descriptions of situations in which there is a misunderstanding, problem, or conflict arising from cultural differences between interacting parties or where there is a problem of cross-cultural adaptation. Each incident gives only enough information to set the stage, describe what happened, and possibly provide the feelings and reactions of the parties involved. It does not explain the cultural differences that the parties bring to the situation. These are discovered or revealed as a part of the exercise (Wright, 1995, p. 128). Benefits include:

- Increases participants' awareness of their own typical, idiosyncratic, or culturally determined interpretations and explanations of others' behavior and their own attitudes and responses in situations such as the ones described;
- Draws out for comparison and analysis of various interpretations and perceptions of participants;
- Clarifies the cultural differences in the incidents that might have contributed to the misunderstandings, problems, and conflicts; and,
- Helps students behave more appropriately and effectively in similar situations. (Wright, 1995, p. 129)

Culture Assimilator/Intercultural Sensitizer: "This instrument is specifically constructed to sensitize persons from one cultural group to the assumptions, behaviors, norms, perceptions, interpretations, attitudes, and values- in short, the subjective culture-of persons from another cultural group" (Triandis as cited in Albert 1995, p. 165). Benefits include:

- Imparts knowledge of the subjective culture of the target group;
- Assists participants develop more accurate expectations in intercultural interactions;
- Helps participants interact more effectively with persons from the target culture;
- Improves knowledge and application of cross-cultural communication concepts; and,
- Increases participants' intercultural sensitivity. (Triandis as cited in Albert, 1995, p. 165)

Case Studies: Case studies are realistic examples of intercultural situations that include "sufficient detail to make it possible for the participants in a training program to analyze the problems involved and to determine possible solutions" (Nadler as cited in Lacey & Trowbridge, 1995, p. 187). Benefits include:

- Reflects the actual complexities of cross-cultural interaction and illustrates that such situations are rarely as simple as they seem;
- Encourages participants to question the notion that there is one right way or one correct answer;
- Helps participants learn to weigh carefully the many factors that affect cross-cultural interaction and to avoid snap judgments that may have negative consequences for the trainee once on the job or in the field; and,
- Encourages students to learn from each other and to appreciate different opinions and is thus particularly effective in a group representing different cultures. (Nadler as cited in Lacey & Trowbridge, 1995, p. 193)

Field Exercises: Field exercises take the students outside the classroom to examine or experience the specified intercultural communication topic in real life. Benefits include:

- Increases their knowledge and behavior by experiencing the actual event outside the classroom;
- Allows students to experience members of other cultures;
- Allows students the opportunity to practice the intercultural communication skills that they have learned in the classroom and from the textbook; and,
- Helps students interact more effectively with members of other cultures.

Media Searches: Media searches take students through all forms of media (papers, films, magazines, television, the arts, etc.) to find examples of the specific concept. Benefits include:

- Students learn the widespread nature of the cultural phenomenon;
- Students come to realize the cultural diversity of the world;
- Students realize the inevitability of cultural contact; and,
- Concepts are applied to the larger social setting and globalization.

SUGGESTIONS FOR POST-EXERCISE DISCUSSIONS

A helpful tool to use when planning an exercise is Covert's (1978) EDIT system. This system suggests that students "**E**xperience" the activity, "**D**escribe" what happened, "**I**nfer" general principles from the activity, and then finally, "**T**ransfer" or apply the principles to their own lives. When discussing the exercise experience with students, Bloom's (1956) taxonomy of educational objectives is helpful for developing different types of questions and bringing students to different stages of awareness. The example below illustrates how this taxonomy can be used to lead a class discussion towards greater levels of higher-order thinking after conducting one case study exercise described in Chapter Two:

Exercise 2.6: Conflicting Messages

(1) *Knowledge*: Describe the interaction between Tim and Raj?
(2) *Understanding*: How did Raj react to Tim's behavior?
(3) *Application*: Have you ever been in a situation when someone perceived you as unfriendly even though you did not feel particularly unfriendly or distant?
(4) *Analysis*: What happens when this occurs in an intercultural situation? What other factors are involved that are not necessarily present in an intracultural situation?
(5) *Evaluation*: Did you think Tim was rude? Do you think Raj overreacted?

Whatever method of questioning you use, any activity should always be discussed or debriefed afterwards in some fashion. A carefully considered list of questions is useful in guiding this discussion.

4

Activities often serve as illustrative catalysts for the more illuminating discussion session that takes place afterwards. It is during these classroom discussions where students come to grips with the concepts illustrated in the activity by verbalizing and sorting through their experience. The post-activity discussion is not merely a quick overview of what happened, with a few substantive comments made only by the teacher. As Nyquist (1979) has stated, an instructional discussion is a developmental process whose "purpose is to move students toward new understanding and appreciation" (p. 7). Students should be talking to each other with the instructor acting as question poser, clarifier, and summarizer.

SAMPLE COURSE SCHEDULES

It is common for instructors to use *Intercultural Communication: A Reader* in conjunction with another intercultural communication textbook. Although the reader can be used alone, undergraduate textbooks in intercultural communication can provide a comprehensive foundation for the study of culture, communication, and intercultural interaction. The course schedules provided on the following pages propose two organizational frameworks for using the *Reader as* the sole reading material in an intercultural communication course. They are intended only as guides and not as completed, ready-to-use course schedules. Your own course objectives, assignments, reading materials, and scheduling preferences must of course be considered when constructing a syllabus and course schedule.

If you are using a textbook in addition to the *Reader*, you will need to modify these frameworks accordingly. Because the course schedules provided include the use of every article in the *Reader*, these schedules will also need to be revised if you plan on using only selected articles. Weekly topic areas and corresponding readings and activities are provided for both a semester and quarter system. The course schedules were developed using the basic organization of the text's eight chapters: (1) Understanding Intercultural Communication, (2) International Cultures, (3) Co-Cultures, (4) Verbal Processes, (5) Nonverbal Processes, (6) Context, (7) Improving Intercultural Communication, and (8) Ethical Considerations.

ORGANIZATION OF A 10-WEEK QUARTER COURSE

Class Period	Content	Weekly Reading	Exercise
Week 1			
1	Introduction to the Course		
2	Understanding Intercultural Communication	Samovar/Porter	1.1, 1.2, 1.3
FILM Bennett 3 *free*	Culture and Conflict	Triandis	1.4
Week 2		*verbal processes*	
4 *5*	Worldview and Intercultural Communication	Ishii, Klopf, Cooke	1.5
5 *6*	Ethnic Paradigms	Janzen	1.6
FILM 6 *7*	Chinese Conceptualizations of Face	Jia	2.1
AMER TONGUES	Korean Patterns of Communication	Robinson	2.2
Week 3			
7 *8*	India: The Dance of Shiva	Gannon	2.3
	Communicating with Egyptians	Begley	2.4
8 *9*	African Cultural Patterns	Van Der Veur	2.5
9 *10*	German and American Managers	Friday	
Week 4			
10	Interethnic Communication	Kim	3,1,3.2
	Black Masculinity	Jackson/Dangerfield	3.3
	Native American Spirituality	Garrett/Wilbur	
11	Communicating With Persons With Disabilities	Braithwaite/ Braithwaite	3.8
	Gay Culture in America	Bronski	3.4
12	Feminine and Masculine Cultures	Wood/Reich	3.5, 3.6
	The Elderly Co-Culture	McKay	3.7
Week 5			
13	Dimensions of Discourse	Johnson	4.5
	Language and Culture	Fong	4.1, 4.6
14	Chinese Language	Zhong	
	Discriminating Attitudes toward Speech	Cargile	4.4, 4.5
15	Mexican Dichos	Roy	4.2, 4.3
	Communication Between Israeli-Jews and Palestinians	Ellis/Maoz	
Week 6			
16	Nonverbal Communication	Andersen	5.1 5.2
	Nonverbal Communication in Japan	McDaniel	5.3, 5.5
17	Monochronic & Polychronic Time	Hall	5.4
18	Gender and Nonverbal Communication	Borisoff/Merrill	5.6, 5.7

Week 7

19	American and Japanese Business Communication	Quasha/McDaniel	6.1, 6.2
	American and Mexican Business Comm.	Lindsley/Braithwaite	6.3
20	Culture and Negotiation	Brett	
	Physician-Patient Communication	Rao	6.4
21	Culture in the Classroom	Gay	6.5

Week 8

22	Intercultural Awareness	Chen/Starosta	7.1, 7.2, 7.3
	Sociocultural Competencies	Mak/Westwood/Ishiyama/Barker	
23	Intercultural Conflicts	Ting-Toomey	7.4
24	Mediating Co-Cultural Conflict	Sauceda	

Week 9

25	Cross-Cultural Adaptation	Begley	7.5, 7.6,7.7
26	Group-Based Tolerance	Baldwin/Hecht	
27	Cultural Identities	Collier	

Week 10

28	Limits to Cultural Diversity	Cleveland	8.1
	Intercultural Personhood	Kim	8.2
	Ethics in Intercultural Communication	Shuter	8.5, 8.6
29	Citizens of the World	Nussbaum	8.3
	Peace as an Ethic for Intercultural Comm.	Kale	8.4
30	Course Summary		

ORGANIZATION OF A 15-WEEK SEMESTER COURSE

Class Period	Content	Weekly Reading	Exercise
Week 1	*Diff approaches*	*A–D*	
1	Introduction to the Course		
2	Understanding Intercultural Communication	Samovar/Porter	1.1, 1.2, 1.3
3	Culture and Conflict	Triandis	1.4,
Week 2			
4	Worldview and Intercultural Communication	Ishii,Klopf,Cooke	1.5
5	Ethnic Paradigms	Janzen	1.6
6	Chinese Conceptualizations of Face	Jia	2.1
Week 3			
7	Korean Patterns of Communication	Robinson	2.2
8	India: The Dance of Shiva	Gannon	2.3
9	Communicating with Egyptians	Begley	2.4
Week 4	*chinese, India*		
10	African Cultural Patterns *?*	Van Der Veur	2.5
11	German and American Managers	Friday	
12	Interethnic Communication	Kim	3.1, 3.2
Week 5			
13	Black Masculinity	Jackson/Dangerfield	3.3
14	Native American Spirituality	Garrett/Wilbur	
15	Communicating with Persons with Disabililities	Braithwaite/Braithwaite	3.8
Week 6			
16	Gay Culture in America	Bronksi	3.4
17	Feminine and Masculine Cultures	Wood/Reich	3.5,3.6
18	The Elderly Co-Culture	McKay	3.7
Week 7			
19	Dimensions of Discourse	Johnson	4.5
20	Language and Culture	Fong	4.1, 4.6
21	Chinese Language	Zhong	
Week 8			
22	Discriminating Attitudes toward Speech	Cargile	4.4, 4.5
23	Mexican *Dichos*	Roy	4.2, 4.3
24	Communication Between Israeli-Jews and Palestinians	Ellis/Maoz	

Bennett — FILM

FILM; AMER TONGUES

Report on "cultural journey"

FILM AND VIDEO RESOURCES

This section includes several film and video resources that connect with and complement many of the articles in the *Reader*. With the literally thousands of titles available to instructors throughout the United States, you should be able to find several nonprint resources to enhance the reading and lecture material in your course. A short, one-sentence description is given for each title and, when available, the year, publisher, and length of the film or video are provided. We urge you to view those films and videos that you are interested in before showing them in your class. Other titles may be found by checking your own school's library reference section and media collection, or conducting a search on the internet. In addition, several titles of film and video locators are provided to help you in your search for instructional media materials.

We encourage you to discuss each film with your students. Students should have an opportunity to talk about what they saw and heard so that concepts and ideas explored in readings, lectures, and exercises may be linked to each film.

Titles

A Clash of Cultures, 1986, 60 min.: Explores African cultural adaptation to outside forces.

Across the Frontiers, 1977, 52 min.: Focuses on the influence of outside forces on tribal societies.

All Under Heaven: Life in a Chinese Village, 1986, 58 min.: Chinese language film (with subtitles) that tells of the history and life of one village in rural China.

American Tongues, 1987, 56 min.: Through interviews with U.S. Americans from many regions of the country, people discuss their attitudes and perceptions of theirs and others' speech.

America--Black and White, NBC, 1981, 75 min.: Through profiles of common citizens, details the serious social and economic situations of African Americans in the U.S.

Asianization of America, 1986, 26 min.: Explores the increasing influence of Asian immigrants to the United States, their influence on the American market, and negative stereotypes which Americans have had toward Asian immigrants.

Being Muslim in India, 1984, 41 min.: A family portrait of a Sunni Muslim and successful businessman in India.

Birthwrite: Growing Up Hispanic, 1989, 60 min.: Through interviews with Latino writers born or raised in the United States of Mexican and Puerto Rican parents, provides insight into the different worlds these writers experienced as children of a minority group.

Black on White, 1986, 58 min.: A film that explores the origins of black English and life in the U.S.

Brazil Hew of South America, 1988, 55 min.: Basic introduction to the people of Brazil, including people of different social, ethnic, and geographic groups.

Bridging the Culture Gap, Copeland Griggs Productions, Inc., 302 23rd Ave., San Francisco, CA 94121 (415) 668-4200, 30 min.: Illustrates the contrasts between North American values and customs with those of cultures throughout the world.

Buddhism, MGHT, 1962, 16 min.: Compares the various sects and beliefs of Buddhism.

Bwana Toshi, ACI Films, 115 min.: Problems encountered by a Japanese volunteer in Kenya.

Christians, Jews and Muslims in Medieval Spain, 1989, 52 min.: Traces the history of Christian, Jewish, and Muslim life in the Iberian peninsula from Roman times through Muslim conquest, through Christian reconquest. Emphasizes unique coexistence.

Communicating Across Cultures, Copeland Griggs Productions, 30 min.: Identifies several ways that culturally different individuals communicate; business context.

Communication- The Nonverbal Agenda, 1988, 20 min.: Discusses the influence that nonverbal cues can have on the meanings of our words.

Differences, Cinema Associates Productions Film, 25 min.: Individuals from different co-cultures relate the difficulties they experience with the dominant culture in the U.S.

Diversity at Work, Copeland Griggs Productions, 30 min.: Shows employees how to work and succeed in the multicultural organization.

Doing Business in Japan- Negotiating a Contract, 1976, 34 min.: Issues that impact the negotiation process (setting, language, interpreter) are examined.

Donahue: Street People, WGN, 1980, 45 min.: Interviews with several homeless people.

Ethnic Notions, 1987, 56 min.: A comprehensive, historical look at cultural stereotypes of African-Americans as portrayed through the U. S. media.

Eye of the Storm, CBS Television, 27 min.: Prejudice in a third grade classroom.

Faces of Change, American Universities Field Staff Films: Focuses on people around the world and their beliefs and values.

Four Families, MGHT, 1965, 60 min.: Focuses on how parents from different cultures raise and interact with their children.

Four Religions, MGHT, 1960, 60 min.: Discusses the beliefs of Hinduism, Buddhism, Islam, and Christianity.

Gefilte Fish, 1984, 15 min.: Cultural changes are represented as three generations of Jewish women prepare Gefilte fish, a traditional holiday dish.

Hard Time, Dave Bell Productions, 1980, 50 min.: Documents life in a maximum security prison-

The Heritage of Slavery, FA, 1968, 54 min.: Examines how the attitudes established during slavery still persist today.

I Am not What You See: Being "Different" In America, 1977, 28 min.: Documents the life of a woman with cerebral palsy who speaks about her experience as a disabled person in the U. S.

I'isaw: Hopi Coyote Stories, 1981, 28 Min.: The social group is represented in the Hopi Indians of Arizona who have been relatively successful in maintaining their land base, language, ceremonies, and cultural identity.

Intercultural Contact, Copeland Griggs Productions, 30 min.: Documents the effects of the Japanese presence in the U.S. through interviews with Japanese and U.S. citizens.

Introduction to American Deaf Cultural Rules of Social Interaction, 1985, 60 min.: Provides an introduction to social interaction among people who are deaf.

Introduction to American Deaf Culture- Values, 1986, 60 min.: Provides an introduction to the unique values and traditions of persons who are deaf.

Invisible Barrier, The, 1979, 18 min.: Examines the stereotype of the disabled including the discomfort of nondisabled persons who meet them for the first time

Language,1988, 55 min. (The Mind Series, Part 7): Explores different theories and ideas about the evolution of human language.

Living Africa: A Village Experience, 1983, 34 min.: Portrays the daily experiences and concerns of the people of Wassetake, a small village on the Senegal River in West Africa.

Managing Differences, Copeland Griggs Productions, 30 min.: Shows managers how to effectively work with a diverse work force.

Mentally Handicapped Children Growing Up: The Brooklands Experiment, 1968, 21 min. Compares the development of children cared for in traditional institutions and small residential treatment programs.

The Five Pillars of Islam, 1988, 30 min.: Explains the major religious principles of Islam.

The Pinks, and the Blues, (Nova), WGBB, 1980, 57 min.: Discusses the socialization process that makes boys and girls "male" and "female."

The Primal Mind, 1983, 58 min.: Explores the basic differences between Native American and Western cultures.

Racism 101, 1988, 58 min.: Documents the racial tension that exploded on the University of Michigan campus after racist jokes were aired.

Radical Sex Styles, (ND), 44 min.: In six candid interviews, examines different approaches to human sexuality including lesbian, gay, bisexual, and transvestite perspectives.

Seven Minute Lesson: Acting as a Sighted Guide, (ND), 7 min.: A guide for sighted people to assist persons with visual impairments in everyday situations.

Sexes: What's the Difference? 1978, 28 min.: Addresses the question of whether or not traits considered "male" and "female" are genetically inherent or learned in childhood.

Taoism: A Question of Balance, Time-Life, 1977, 52 min.: Discusses the religious beliefs of the Taiwanese.

The Rice Ladle- The Changing Role of Women in Japan, 1981, 28 min.: Explores the changing roles of women in Japan.

The Turning Points, WPBT-TV, Miami, 1973, 29 min.: Discusses the phenomenon of growing old in youthful America.

Wages of Action, 1979, 47 min.: A description of life in a Hindu village and how the Hindu religion touches each aspect.

We're Moving Up: The Hispanic Migration, NBC, 1980, 81 min.: Discusses the population and socioeconomic changes of the Latino people; values, cultural characteristics, and historical information are addressed.

Women in a Changing World, American Universities Field Staff Films, 48 min.: Women from around the world discuss issues of global concern.

Working in the U.S.A, Copeland Griggs Productions, 30 min.: Describes the values and dynamics of the U.S. workplace.

Yo Soy, 1985, 60 min.: Documents the progress that Chicanos have made in politics, education, labor, and economic development in the past two decades.

Film and Video Locators

AID Catalog of Films, Agency for Economic Development's Training Office, USAID Library, 1621 North Kent Street, Rosslyn, VA 22209. (Films on Third World and non-Western countries only.)

Cortes, C. E., & Campbell, L. G. (I 979). Race and ethnicity in the history of the Americas: A filmic approach. Riverside, CA: Latin American Studies Program, University of California, Riverside, 92521.

The Educational Film Locator, Consortium of University Film Center. (Available in major libraries.)

Tricontinental Film Center, Third World Cinema, P.O. Box 4430, Berkeley, CA. UNESCO Publications Centre, P.O. Box 433, New York, NY 100 1 6.

The 1986 Video Sourcebook, National Video Clearinghouse, I 00 Lafayette Drive, Syosset, NY 11791.

Helpful Sources for Compiling these Film and Video Resources

Asuncion-Lunde, N. C. (nd). Intercultural communication: Teaching strategies, resources and materials. Unpublished paper.

Directory of selected resources. (1988). Portland, OR: Intercultural Communication Institute.

Educational media collection. (1991). Seattle: Instructional Media Services, University of Washington.

Kohls, L. R., & Tyler, V. L. (1988). Area studies resources, Provo, UT: David M. Kennedy Center for International Studies, Brigham Young University.

Samovar, L. A., & Stefani, L. A. (November, 1995). Teaching the intercultural communication course at the college and university level. A short course conducted for the Speech Communication Association Convention, San Antonio, TX.

Samovar, L. A., & Stefani, L. A. (November, 1994). Teaching the intercultural communication course at the college and university level. Short course conducted for the Speech Communication Association, New Orleans, LA.

Schmidt, W. V., Freeman, J. B., Samovar, L. A., Kim, Y. Y., & Dodd, C. H. (November, 1984). Teaching the college course: Intercultural communication. A workshop presented at the convention of the Speech Communication Association, Chicago.

Stevens, G. 1. (1993). Videos for understanding diversity. Chicago: American Library Association.

INTERNET RESOURCES

The internet has provided new opportunities for students to learn about other cultures. It is itself a place with much cultural diversity and offers teachers and students new resources to study intercultural communication. A search for intercultural resources on the internet can be easily done by using any of the major search engines. This list of resources will only highlight some of the more interesting kinds of web sites that you can use to help you and your students teach and learn intercultural communication. The internet has become so user-friendly that the most effective and efficient way to find information on intercultural communication topics is to do an individual search on a particular country, culture, religion, language, etc. One word of caution, however, if you are asking students to do research reports on various cultures. University students have become so accustomed to using *only* the Web to access information for research that they forget about other kinds of information that university libraries typically hold. Remind them of that ancient form of communication called "the book." Books are still the most plentiful source of information available on other cultures.

- **Intercultural Communication LOOP**. According to this website at <http://www.webcom.com/lbdavies/intercultural/icclwelcome.html>, "The Intercultural Communication LOOP is your connection to the best Intercultural Communication sites on the Web. The only requirement to join this LOOP is that the site you submit be related to intercultural communication...This is a multilingual LOOP, and all sites are welcome...The Intercultural Communication LOOP works like this: Each site is linked to the next in a circular fashion. The user can navigate around the Intercultural Communication LOOP until s/he finally ends up back at the beginning."

- **University Websites**. Students could learn a great deal about intercultural communication by surveying university websites in different countries. For example, B'Not Torah Institute at http://www.bti.org.il/ for orthodox Jewish women provides information not just on university programs but includes essays written by members of the Institute. Such essays can provide valuable insight into the values, beliefs, and ways of communicating in other countries and cultures. A simple search of "Yahoo!" under "Education: Universities" provides an enormous list of countries with university websites.

- **Government/Embassy Websites**. It is common for even the smallest countries to have an official national website that includes information for tourists and others interested in finding out more about the country. For example, Namibia has an official website at <http://www.republicofnamibia.com/> and Jordan has two official government websites at <http://www.kinghussein.gov.jo/> (the late King Hussein's personal website) and <http://www.noor.gov.jo/QNoorjo/> (personal website of Queen Noor).

- **Regional and Culture-Specific Sites**. There are some websites that are devoted to providing information on a specific region, culture, religion, or country. For example, Arab Net at <http://www.arab.net/> is an excellent first-stop website for finding information about virtually every Islamic country in the world. And Hindu Resources On-line at <http://www.hindu.org/> provides countless links to Hindu-related websites.

- **Intercultural/Cross-cultural Training Organizations**. A large group of training organizations can be accessed by doing a search using the search term "intercultural communication" on "Yahoo!" or "Excite!" For example, The Centre For International Briefing at <http://www.cibfarnham.com/> provides country specific briefings, intercultural workshops, and language training for international managers. And the Intercultural Management Institute at <http://www.imi.american.edu/> describes services that include cross-cultural orientation and negotiations, multicultural management, and US business culture training. Consider asking students to do a research project that includes surveying intercultural training and consulting organizations and reporting on common practices and recent trends.

- **International Chat Rooms**. One way to provide students with more experiential learning opportunities is to have them join a chat room focused on a particular language, culture, or country. An "Excite" search using the term "international chat rooms" reaped 20 sites, including: "Aftonbladet Chat," a Swedish chat room at <http://chat.aftonbladet.se/>; "Nihongo Chat," a Japanese-English chat room at <http://www.nihongo.org/english/chat/>; and "Cippolin@ Talk System," an Italian chat network at <http://chat.onion.it/cipollina.html>. Do remind your students, however, that they need to proceed with caution as they enter and begin to converse in an on-line chat room. This kind of intercultural communication doesn't have the benefit of face-to-face interaction and they should exercise good sense and discretion as they chat.

References for Introduction

Albert, R. D. (1995). The intercultural sensitizer/cultural assimilator as a cross-cultural training method. In S. M. Fowler & M. G. Mumford (Eds.), <u>Intercultural sourcebook: Cross-cultural training methods, Vol. 1</u>. Yarmouth, Maine: Intercultural Press.

Bloom, B. S. (1956). <u>Taxonomy of educational objectives: Cognitive domain</u>. New York: David McKay Co.

Covert, A. (1978). <u>Communication: "People speak" instructor's manual</u>. New York: McGraw-Hill.

Lacey, L. & Trowbridge, J. (1995). Using the case study as a training tool. In S. M. Fowler & M. G. Mumford (Eds.), <u>Intercultural sourcebook: Cross-cultural training methods, Vol. I</u>. Yarmouth, Maine: Intercultural Press.

McCaffery, J. A. (1995). The role play: A powerful but difficult training tool. In S. M. Fowler & M. G. Mumford (Eds.), <u>Intercultural sourcebook: Cross-cultural training methods, Vol. I</u>. Yarmouth, Maine: Intercultural Press.

Nyquist, J. L. (1979). <u>The instructional discussion method</u>. Seattle: University of Washington.

Nyquist L., & Wulff, D. H. (1990). Selected active learning strategies. In J. Daly, G. Friedrich, & A. Vangelisti (Eds.), <u>Teaching communication: Methods, research, and theory</u>, Hillsdale, NJ: Lawrence Erlbaum.

Sisk, D. A. (I 995). Simulation games as training tools. In S. M. Fowler & M. G. Mumford (Eds.), <u>Intercultural sourcebook: Cross-cultural training methods, Vol. I</u>, Yarmouth, Maine: Intercultural Press.

Wright, A. R. (I 995). The critical incident as a training tool. In S. M. Fowler & M. G.

CHAPTER RESOURCES

This section of the manual provides suggestions for using each chapter of the *Reader*. We have included the following for each chapter: chapter synopsis, class discussion questions, exercises, and test questions. Each chapter synopsis identifies primary concepts or questions that your students should be able to identify and answer after reading the articles in the chapter. The discussion questions provide ways to engage your students in an in-depth, thought-provoking discussion on issues related to ideas expressed in each chapter. Each discussion question is focused on central ideas from one article.

The exercises provided are of three primary types: reflective, experiential, and case studies. The reflective exercises often ask students to work alone or in groups and consider their own feelings about a particular topic related to intercultural communication. These exercises can also be used as take-home assignments. The experiential exercises ask students to "do" intercultural communication in either simulated or authentic situations. And finally, the case studies provided for each chapter ask students to consider examples of intercultural communication and identify the primary issues, problems, and solutions for each one. All exercises include questions to facilitate small group and/or whole class discussion. Finally, each chapter ends with multiple choice, true/false, and essay test items for each article.

Part 1
Intercultural Interaction: An Introduction

Chapter 1
Approaches To Understanding Intercultural Communication

Chapter Synopsis

This chapter introduces the topic of intercultural communication and provides a spectrum of approaches to culture, communication, and interactions between cultures. Your students should be able to answer four broad questions about intercultural communication after reading the articles in this chapter: (1) What is intercultural communication? (2) How do cultures differ communicatively? (3) What influences and/or impedes intercultural understanding? (4) What contributes to one's worldview?

Samovar and Porter argue for the importance of intercultural communication. Their article provides an introduction, both to the basic components of culture, and to the core ideas of intercultural communication. Triandis' article reviews two ways which culture is related to conflict: cultural distance and cultural syndromes. Triandis introduces ten cultural syndromes that he then relates to the situation, communication and conflict. Ishii, Klopf, and Cooke discuss how the concept of worldview shapes culture. Elements of worldview are provided as well as types of worldviews. Religion plays a fundamental role in shaping one's worldview. Numerous examples are provided to allow students to examine various religious worldviews.

Finally, Janzen's article identifies five different paradigms in which Americans in general define ethnic relations. Beginning with Traditional Eurocentric Racism and ending with Centered Pluralism, Janzen traces the history of Multiculturalism. This article clearly identifies the assumptions, values, and goals of each paradigm. Janzen challenges the students to pay particular attention to the philosophical positions and perceptions of the numerous representatives of Multiculturalism in order to understand how the different paradigms affect intercultural communication.

Discussion Ideas

1. Why should we study intercultural communication?
    a. Ask students to list spontaneously their reasons for taking an intercultural communication course. What do they hope to get out of the course? What are the benefits? Why even have such a course? List their responses on the chalkboard.
    b. Ask students to give their answers. Play the "devil's advocate" and encourage students to elaborate on their reasons. For example, a common response to why we should study intercultural communication is that it will increase intercultural understanding among peoples of the world and help people get along. One response to this answer is that not everyone wants to communicate with people who are culturally dissimilar and what really are the benefits of such interactions? Hasn't communication been known to strain rather than improve intercultural relations? Why can't we just stay in our own communities and communicate with the people who are like us? Such a response can spark further dialogue on the inevitability of intercultural contact, as well as force students to challenge the assumption that communication always and necessarily improves understanding.
    c. Finally, ask students to give one way that their lives could change as a result of taking an intercultural communication course. How will they have changed their lives or ways of thinking and communicating with culturally dissimilar individuals after the course has ended? Encourage students to be specific about these changes and have them write the changes down on a card and refer back to them at the end of the term.

2. Is perception strictly a physiological process? To what degree is perception influenced by one's culture? Is all perception really culturally and individually based? Isn't there such a thing as "fact" or "objective reality"? Can't we agree that many things about the world just are? Given all this, how are we to understand perception? This question encourages students to think of perception as a series of complex and sometimes contradictory processes, rather than an automatic function of being human.

3. What are some characteristics of collectivist cultures? What are some characteristics of individualist cultures? How do these characteristics differ? Have students identify classmates or friends who exhibit these characteristics. Then have students identify whether they belong to individualist cultures or collectivist cultures. What cultures do they believe to be individualist? Collectivist?

4. Which researchers worldview do students most identify? Why? This can provide a discussion to determine why some students believe in certain things while others have different beliefs, values, etc. Are these beliefs based in their worldview? Is their identification with this worldview related to their own culture? How does their worldview contribute to their culture?

5.   Using the Interethnic Relationships paradigm chart provided by Janzen as a starting point, have students identify historical antecedents that have caused a shift in the five categories across paradigms. This will help students understand that history, context, and situations affect perceptions of ethnic relations. From their experiences in school, work, and life in general, in which paradigm would they classify most Americans? Is there a majority? Is there a progressive trend toward adopting paradigm V? Will new paradigms emerge as current ones become inadequate? What might they be? How do these paradigms affect intercultural communication?

Exercises

Exercise 1.1: Intercultural Communication Model. This exercise asks students to construct their own model of the intercultural communication process based on those elements they feel most influences an intercultural interaction. Students will apply the knowledge they have learned in Chapter 1 to their own experiences as intercultural communicators. Briefly review the elements of intercultural communication as outlined in the article by Samovar and Porter. Then divide the class into groups of 4-6 students. Ask students to illustrate intercultural communication by constructing a model of the process. Each group should decide which elements of intercultural communication they will include in their model. Suggest to the students that they use their own interactions with culturally different peoples as frameworks for choosing their model's components. For example, some students may have experienced an intercultural situation where language was a barrier in the interaction.   Others may have noticed particular nonverbal behaviors that were markedly different than their own. Also stress to students that they should think of the basic process of communication as discussed in other courses they've taken in communication.

Ask each group to present its model using a hypothetical intercultural interaction as an [DIALOG or SKIT] example that shows how the model works in "real life". If students are given enough time, some groups may choose to develop a skit to illustrate their model. Each group should state the respective cultures of the interactants, the scene (in a restaurant, on a date, in a classroom, etc.), and the affiliation level of the dyad (strangers, acquaintances, friends, lovers, etc.). The following questions are offered to stimulate discussion. How did you come up with these components? Which components do you feel most impact intercultural communication? Why? Which components do you feel pose the biggest challenge for interactants? The least challenge? How are the components of the communication process affected by the added variable of culture? Can any component of the communication process escape culture's influence?

Exercise 1.2: How Others Perceive Us. This exercise asks students to imagine how others might perceive them culturally and individually in an intercultural interaction. The objective of this activity is to make students aware of how others might perceive them in an intercultural setting and how closely these perceptions match students' own perceptions of their cultural and personal characteristics. Have students answer the following two questions individually. Impress upon them that they are to imagine, as much as possible, how others would perceive them, not how they perceive themselves. It might be helpful for students if they would imagine an intercultural encounter that they have had previously.

a.   List 10 cultural predictions that you think others would use to describe you in an intercultural interaction.

b.   List 10 individual predictions that you think others would use to describe you in an intercultural interaction.

Afterwards, the class may either be separated into small discussion groups or a large class discussion may follow. Have students share some of their answers. Possible questions for discussion might be: Where might people get these cultural and individual characteristics? How accurate would their impressions of you be if these were the only predictions they could make about you? What errors would they make? Do you think that their impression is the "real" you? How similar are their cultural and individual predictions? How different are they? Where are the contradictions? In what situations do you think it would be useful to make strictly cultural predictions? Only individual predictions? When are both most useful? Should people only assess others based on perceived individual characteristics?

Like BANGA →

Exercise 1.3: Interactional Rules. This exercise includes aspects from all the articles in Chapter 1. Specifically, it illustrates how communication is so strongly rule-governed and yet we follow these rules unconsciously. By taking part in a cross-cultural simulation activity, students will gain insight into the difficulty that arises when two culture-specific rule systems are used in an intercultural interaction. Divide the class into two groups, the Sopa culture and the Epa culture. Each group should receive handouts with culture-specific rules that will govern its behavior when it interacts with the other (rules are provided as handouts on the next two pages). Give students the rules one class period before the day that the game is to be played. This will ensure that each student will be adequately prepared to take part in the simulation. Tell students not to share their group's rules with any member of the other group. The success of this game hinges on each team not being explicitly aware of the rules that govern the other group's behavior.

After students have been given adequate preparation time to learn the rules of their assigned cultures, have the two groups take part in a twenty-minute interaction session. You may set up a scene where the two groups will negotiate a business transaction or a party where there are both social and business conversations taking place. You could even provide some refreshments to make a party scene more realistic. Some students from the same culture may wish to pair up as friends, lovers, students, siblings, a married couple, or business partners.

After the two cultures have interacted, have the students write for five minutes on the following questions: What specific behaviors of the other culture did you notice? What social rules do you think were governing these behaviors?

As with all cross-cultural simulations, a class discussion should follow. Students should come away from this discussion with an understanding of some of the cultural rules that guide their own daily interactions and the impact that interactional rules have on intercultural communication. Each of the articles in Chapter 1 is relevant to this exercise. Some possible questions to stimulate discussion: What were some of the difficulties you experienced in preparing for this interaction? Which rules of your "adopted culture" conflicted with the rules of your "true" culture? When did you begin to catch on to some of their social rules? What was one of the first things you noticed about how the other culture behaved? What was your initial internal reaction? What was your external reaction to this behavior? How did you (or why didn't you) modify your behavior to compensate for the other culture's rules? What were some of the most difficult moments during your interactions? What were some of the most enjoyable? Did successful communication take place? What information about the other culture do you wish you had been given before your interaction? What information about your own culture could be given to other cultures to aid them in their interactions with you?

Exercise 1.3: Interactional Rules

Rules for the Sopa Culture

Sopas are extremely social, but their socializing is dictated by the women. Men can speak freely with other men, but must be restrained in contact with women. This matriarchal society is also highly materialistic. A major source of conversation is derived from discussing each other's material assets.

Example of greeting: Hi Jimmy! How's your new radial tire?

Keep in mind the following social rules:

A. **Initiating Conversation**. Always begin social contact with a materialistic statement. Inquiries into each other's financial situation are considered proper etiquette.

B. **Degree of Verbalization**. Constant verbalizing is a sign of successful communication. Perpetual chitchat is critical both in social and business interactions.

C. **Sex Roles**. Women must remember to protect their males from strangers. If a stranger stands too close to a male member, intercept without speaking.

D. **Nonverbal Behavior**.

Touching: Each touches the other, except handshaking is considered an insult. Men must wait to be touched by women before they can reciprocate.

Gestures: The right hand is considered an evil and disgusting part of the human anatomy. It must never contact a human or be used in giving something to another. Right palm facing a person is an obscene gesture.

Eye Contact: Women engage in sustained eye contact. Men lower their eyes when speaking to women or strangers.

Facial Gestures: Wetting one's lips with the tongue is considered a very provocative or complimentary gesture to be used ONLY when one wishes to "charm" the opposite sex. Tongue rolling is a definite attempt at hustling. (Gestures can be used by both sexes.)

E. **Business**. This highly materialistic society thinks of business as merely an extension of their social life, only more aggressive. Although men can initiate a sale, ONLY WOMEN CAN BARTER and complete the transaction.

Exercise 1.3: Interactional Rules

Rules for the Epa Culture

Epas believe in the separateness of the self from others. If possible, they would live in isolated cells, but since they form a group, they make all attempts to cooperate while minimizing self-revelation. Epas are themselves only part of the natural cycle and, therefore, hold nature as sacred as humans. They speak *through* nature so all communication is a metaphor.

> Example: This rose is wilting. (I am tired.)
> Does the cow sit at your table? (Do you eat meat?)
> How are the saplings in your forest? (How is your family?)

Keep in mind the following social rules:

A.   **Initiating Conversation**. Always begin social contact with reference to the weather or other natural phenomena.

B.   **Degree of Verbalization**. The ability to use metaphorical language is an art form that establishes a type of caste system. Clear, moderately slow speech production punctuated with intermittent silence to enable aesthetic appreciation is a sign of articulate communication.

C.   **Sex Roles**. Within the culture an asexual attitude prevails. Members tend to find other cultures very exciting but strangers sometimes misunderstand the treatment of sex and "nature's function".

D   **Nonverbal Behavior**.

Touching: Epas are essentially aphysical and, therefore, avoid touching one another. An interesting feature in this culture is that individuals seem to touch and hold themselves (i.e., arm folding, face touching, etc.) a lot. Positive sentiment is expressed in flowery metaphorical language.

Gestures: Yes/agreement/happiness—signified by touching chin to chest (rapid chin touching = great excitement/vigorous agreement). No/disagreement/disgust--rolling the shoulders. "Say again" or repeat--is indicated by touching your fist to your forehead.

Facial Gestures: The human tongue is considered a disgusting part of the human anatomy. Showing your tongue or pointing a finger are considered GRAVE insults.

E.   **Business**. The following only relate to business negotiations:

1.   All trading is done standing.
2.   Women cannot touch money.

Exercise 1.4: Collectivist and Individualist Cultures.

This exercise will help students understand the characteristics of both collectivist and individualist cultures. Divide the class into two groups. Ask students in one group to identify characteristics of collectivist cultures. Ask students in the second group to identify characteristics of individualist cultures. Then have students list which characteristics they can identify as part of their own culture. Are these characteristics those identified as being part of a collectivist or an individualist culture?

Exercise 1.5: East vs. West

This exercise will allow students to clearly differentiate between the East/West Dichotomy as outlined by Gilgen and Cho (1979) in Ishii, Klopf, and Cooke. More importantly students will be provided an opportunity to understand both dichotomies. Divide the class in two groups. Designate one group to represent the East and the other to represent the West. Using the East/West Dichotomy have students provide an example of each of the characteristics as outlined on page 30 of the textbook. Then ask all students to explain which worldview they can relate to and why. Specifically why could they live under the beliefs of the one worldview versus another.

Exercise 1.6: Philosophical Positions, Perceptions, and Intercultural Communication.

This exercise will help students better understand the five paradigms identified by Janzen and how they affect perceptions and intercultural communication. Divide the students into groups of two or three and have them pick a paradigm they are interested in. Have them first identify one or more underlying assumption(s) of the paradigm. Next have them interview five people regarding the assumption(s). For example, an underlying assumption of Centered Pluralism is that in order for America to hold itself together as a national system, there must be certain central traditions that are adhered to by most citizens. Have them interview five people and ask them what common traditions (if any) there should be for all Americans. Finally, students can report their findings as well as their own views to the rest of the class incorporating the impact on intercultural communication.

Test Items for Chapter 1

Multiple Choice

1.   According to Samovar and Porter, which of the following are NOT among the events that have led to the development of the global village?
        a.   globalization of the economy
        b.   changes in immigration patterns
        c.   developments in communication technology
        d.   increased intercultural understanding *

2.   Improvements in communication technology have produced many effects worldwide. Which of the following effects is among the most significant to intercultural communication?
        a.   immediacy of new communication technology *
        b.   increased television watching and decreased interpersonal interactions
        c.   tendency to objectify people
        d.   stronger value of materialism worldwide

3.   What is the basic function of culture?
        a.   To help people deal with problems
        b.   To describe a predictable world in which the individual is firmly rooted
        c.   To make sense of surroundings and ease transitions
        d.   All of the above *

4.   Culture is
        a.   static.
        b.   innate.
        c.   random.
        d.   learned. *

5.   Which of the following are "teachers" of American culture?
        a.   The saying, "the squeaky wheel gets the grease."
        b.   A mother telling her son, "Dress up is for girls, honey."
        c.   a & b *
        d.   none of the above

6.   According to Samovar and Porter's introduction, cultures are
        a.   highly adaptive and, therefore, undergo complete change with every generation.
        b.   dynamic and, therefore, do not retain any particular characteristics over time.
        c.   highly adaptive, yet possess a deep structure that resists major alterations. *
        d.   do not exist in a vacuum, yet remain static over time.

7. *"Nearly always the folklore of a people includes myths of origin which give priority to themselves, and place the stamp of supernatural approval upon their particular customs"* (10). This statement by Keesing (1965) best illustrates which of the following characteristics of culture?
   a. culture is learned
   b. culture is transmitted from generation to generation
   c. culture is based on symbols
   d. culture is ethnocentric *

8. Which characteristic of culture most directly relates to intercultural communication according to Samovar and Porter?
   a. culture is based on symbols
   b. culture is ethnocentric *
   c. culture is subject to change
   d. culture is learned

9. What are the two dominant social organizations found in a culture?
   a. political affiliation and club memberships
   b. workplace and peer group
   c. school and family *
   d. ethnicity and community identification

10. Silence, eye contact, and handshakes are all forms of what kind of communication?
    a. nonverbal *
    b. paralinguistic
    c. conscious
    d. intentional

11. In collectivist cultures people are more likely
    a. to sample the collective self rather than to sample the individual self
    b. to give more priority to the goals of their in-group than to their personal goals
    c. to use in-group norms to shape their behavior more than personal attitudes
    d. all of the above *

12. Which of the following is not considered an individualist culture?
    a. North American
    b. Australia
    c. New Zealand
    d. Latin American *

13. Which of the following is not characteristic of those in an individualist culture?
    a. sample the individual self
    b. use norms much more than attitudes as determinants of their social behavior *
    c. pay attention to their own needs only and abandon interpersonal relationships
    d. give priority to personal goals

14. Which of the following assumes, "When people come into contact with members of other cultures, they are often not aware of their miscommunications, because they think that the others are more or less like they are"?
    a. conscious incompetence
    b. unconscious incompetence *
    c. conscious competence
    d. unconscious competence

15. Which of the following assumes, "After some interpersonal difficulties people realize that they are miscommunicating, but they do not know exactly what is wrong"?
    a. conscious incompetence *
    b. unconscious incompetence
    c. conscious competence
    d. unconscious competence

16. In the West communication is typically
    a. abstractive *
    b. associative
    c. neither a or b
    d. none of the above

17. Factors that have been found to increase aggression include
    a. biological factors
    b. social structural factors
    c. modeling
    d. all of the above *

18. The rejection of out-groups is especially like to occur in
    a. collectivist cultures *
    b. individualist cultures
    c. both a and b
    d. none of the above

19. Which of the following is not a belief of the West Worldview?
    a. Humans are separate from nature and overshadowed by a personal God
    b. Humans consist of mind, body, and soul.
    c. Humans are one with nature, they should feel comfortable with anyone. *
    d. Humans have to manipulate and control nature to survive.

20. Which researcher(s) places stress on religion in developing worldview?
    a. Helve
    b. Rubin and Peplau
    c. Samovar and Porter
    d. Emerson *

21. Which of the following does Helve (1991) not consider a part of worldview?
    a. scientific
    b. metaphysical
    c. religious
    d. educational *

22. According to the Traditional Eurocentric Racism Paradigm (1):
    a. America was characterized by a dominant Orthodox Christian tradition.
    b. All Europeans, despite their religious affiliation, experienced no discrimination.
    c. Non-Europeans, such as American Indians, Blacks, Asians, and Mexicans, were all considered inferior peoples and were never fully accepted as Americans. *
    d. Protestant, Catholic, Christian, and Jewish religions were readily accepted.

23. Janzen indicates that in the melting pot paradigm (II),
    a. rather than melting equally into American society, immigrants had to shed their traditional cultural beliefs and practices in favor of "American" ones. *
    b. all immigrant groups retained their own languages.
    c. marrying across ethnic boundaries was prohibited.
    d. we find an accurate account of what actually transpired in American history.

24. Which paradigm advocates the creation and maintenance of semi-independent or separate ethnic groups within the U.S.?
    a. Globalism (IV)
    b. Ethnic Nationalism (III) *
    c. Central Pluralism (V)
    d. Traditional Eurocentric Racism (I)

25. According to Janzen,
   a.   all five paradigms are present in today's society. *
   b.   these five paradigms make solutions to social problems easier.
   c.   it is easy to identify the "real" multiculturalists.
   d.   the last three paradigms have leveled the playing field for most ethnic groups.

True/False

F	1.	The globalization of the economy has had little impact on intercultural communication among the world's people.
T	2.	Intercultural communication occurs whenever a message produced in one culture must be processed in another culture.
T	3.	A basic function of culture is to help us make sense of our surroundings.
T	4.	The deep structure of a culture (i.e., values, morals, religious practices) rarely changes because it is able to resist major alterations.
F	5.	Culture is the internal process by which we select, evaluate, and organize stimuli from the external environment.
T	6.	Values are like rules that proscribe behaviors expected of a culture's members.
F	7.	More than anything else, differences in language isolate cultures and cause them to regard each other as strange.
T	8.	Western individualist cultures sample mostly the *content* of communications.
F	9.	Conflict is greater when two cultures are very similar than when they are very different.
T	10.	A cultural syndrome is a shared pattern of beliefs, attitudes, self-definitions, norms, roles, and values organized around a theme.
F	11.	In collectivist cultures people pay attention to the needs of others and stay in relationships even when that is not maximally beneficial to them.
F	12.	The four aspects of collectivists cultures are not interrelated.
T	13.	Collectivists use action verbs rather than state verbs.
T	14.	Conformity is high in tight cultures.
T	15.	Hollywood stars live in a culture that is both complex and loose.
F	16.	In the West conformity is seen as something that is desirable.
T	17.	Vertical cultures accept hierarchy as a given.
T	18.	Worldview distinguishes one culture from another.
T	19.	Worldview consists of the most general and comprehensive concepts and unstated assumptions about life.
T	20.	Many melting pot theorists today call themselves "multiculturalists".
F	21.	Paradigm II suggests the blending together of all original ethnic cultures and traditions.
F	22.	The Melting Pot Paradigm presents an accurate account of what actually transpired in American history.
F	23.	Centered Pluralism is much less prescriptive in nature than globalism.

T   24.   Centered Pluralism assumes an underlying commitment to the kind of general principles enunciated in the United States Constitution's Bill of Rights.

T   25.   The Traditional Eurocentric paradigm (I) and the Melting Pot paradigm (II) are both assimilationist paradigms.

T   26.   The paradigms of Ethnic Nationalism (III), Globalism (IV), and Centered Pluralism (V), all seek the retention and maintenance of traditional cultural beliefs and practice.

F   27.   According to Centered Pluralism, all ethnicities contribute to a rapidly changing American character.

T   28.   Globalism asks us to think in terms of foundations that might hold all cultures of the world together.

Essay Questions

1.   Describe an intercultural communication interaction that you have experienced using the four characteristics of communication as identified by Samovar and Porter.

2.   Describe how the mechanisms of invention and diffusion produce change in a culture.

3.   Identify, define, and give an example of each of the six characteristics of culture as explained by Samovar and Porter. Would you add a characteristic that they do not include?

4.   Describe how beliefs, values, and attitudes are interrelated and their relation to communication.

5.   How are cultural and intercultural competence different? How are they related?

6.   Explain how the following proverb relates the link between family and how we communicate with other people: "The apple does not fall far from the tree."

7.   Of the ten cultural syndromes outlined in Triandis' article on Culture and Conflict, which of the syndromes most closely relate to a culture of which you are a member? Identify the culture syndrome and provide an example of specifically how the culture you belong to correspond with the syndrome.

8.   Differentiate between "tight" and "loose" cultures.

9.   When people come into contact with members of other cultures they communicate through various stages. Briefly review these stages and how they are important in the communication process.

10.   Explain the statement, "All humans are ethnocentric".

11.   Identify Redfield's (1953) general conceptions of the elements of worldview.

12.   Ten characteristics can be generated from Pennington's (1985) conception of worldview elements. Identify and explain five of those characteristics.

13.   Explain the East-West dichotomy worldview as described by psychologists Gilgen and Cho (1979).

14.   Explain Dodd's (1987) worldview elements.

15.   Differentiate between Helve's (1991) three types of worldviews: scientific, metaphysical and religious.

16. Ruyard Kipling's famous words, "Oh, East is East, and West is West, and never the twain shall meet" can be used to describe the colliding worldviews of the East and the West. Compare and Contrast these two views.

17. Samovar, Porter and Stefani (1998) identify five similarities of Eastern and Western religions. Identify, define, and give an example of each of the similarities.

18. Explain why Janzen calls the Globalism (IV) paradigm a "Star Trek vision."

19. Describe the primary differences between the Traditional Eurocentric Racism (I), Melting Pot (II) paradigms and the Ethnic Nationalism (III), Globalism (IV), Centered Pluralism (V) paradigms.

20. Describe the historical nature of culture as discussed by Samovar & Porter. How do these authors support the statement, "Culture is historically transmitted"?

21. Using information and examples from each of the articles in Part One of the *Reader,* describe how culture is like a "screen" that allows individuals to attend to only certain stimuli and ignore all others.

22. Using information from each of the articles in Part One, identify some of the ways culture is "subtle."

23. Using information from each of the articles in Part One, answer the following questions: What does it mean to communicate interculturally? What must people consider when they communicate interculturally?

Part 2
Sociocultural Backgrounds: What We Bring to Intercultural Communication

Chapter 2
International Cultures: Understanding Diversity

Chapter Synopsis

Chapter 2 focuses on cultures around the world and how their worldviews and belief and value systems influence their communication. Students will be challenged with the following four questions about intercultural communication after reading this chapter: (1) What cultural differences exist between Eastern and Western peoples? (2) How do these differences influence their ways of communicating? (3) What are the different modes and methods of persuasion valued and practiced by different cultures? (4) How do different cultures conceive of interpersonal conflict and struggle, and why does conflict pervade the everyday lives of members of some cultures and be avoided at all costs in others?

Jia's article examines the Chinese concept of face. Learning about the concept of face will allow students to obtain a closer look into the Chinese culture. Robinson's article explores the Korean concept of *nunch'i*, a communicative practice that involves using the eyes to perceive the world and to read the eyes of others. Students should be able to trace the influence of Confucianism—on *nunch'i* practice and sensibility. Perhaps most valuable are the anecdotes offered by the author to illustrate effective and ineffective interactions with *nunch'i*.

Gannon examines Hindu traditions for they are an integral part of the Indian culture. He explores the "Dance of Shiva" as a means to understand Hindu religion. This dance symbolizes the five main activities of the supreme being. Because the culture of Africa is so vast, Van Der Veur's essay reviews those communication and cultural patterns evident in Africa South of the Sahara. By reading this article students can become more informed about the communication and cultural patterns of Africa.

Begley focuses on Egyptian worldview and religion, values, and language because she understands these to be the most influential cultural characteristics in communication situations between Egyptians and non-Egyptians. Her article anticipates and challenges some of the preconceptions American students might have about Egyptian culture. As the leader of such a discussion, the instructor may want to use the distinctions between these two Eastern religions to challenge the notions of East and West as monolithic categories.

In the final article Friday looks at the different discussion behaviors of German and American managers in order to show the "real life" consequences of cultural difference in international business relations.

These articles will help the students understand that members from different cultures bring different histories and worldviews to a communication event and these differences impact and influence interaction.

Discussion Ideas

1.   How would relationship development differ among people who value *being* versus *doing?* Ask students to describe a person who values a "being" perspective of life and one who values a "doing" perspective. Are such persons so different that they could not form a satisfying interpersonal relationship or communicate effectively?

2.   What kind of communication would ensue between a person who has a process, receiver view of communication and a person who has an outcome, sender view of communication? What are the differences in perception that these two people must overcome if they are to communicate effectively? Is it enough just to know that each has a different view of communication or must adjustments be made? (This raises the issue of whether "just knowing" about differences in communication is enough. Usually it is not.) If adjustments need to be made, ask students to consider what those adjustments might be.

3.   What is *nunch'i?* How does *nunch'i* reflect the Confucian value of self-control? How does *nunch'i* help those less powerful to negotiate hierarchical relationships? How does the Korean priority of harmony make for different communicative ethics than ours in America?

4.   What kind of American does Robinson seem to be addressing? What does this imply about American communicative ethics? What are the ethical stakes in learning *nunch'i* in order to perform business transactions with Koreans? Should Americans be taught *nunch'i* just so they can become more successful in business negotiations with Koreans? Or should there be a more "humanistic," less profit-motivated goal behind learning such a culture-specific communication practice? Robinson's article is an excellent opportunity to discuss motivation and purpose behind learning about other cultures and their unique ways of communicating.

5.   How would the Hindu view of life, the world, and salvation influence communication between Hindus and non-Hindus?
     a.   Ask students to first describe in their own words the various beliefs of the Hindu religion. Record their responses on the chalkboard by labeling separate columns as "life," "world," and "salvation."

b. Next, ask them to take another culture that they have read about (the Germans or Chinese, for example) and describe how people from these cultures would view these same three topics

c. With the two sets of cultural beliefs on the board, ask students to reflect on how two people from these two cultures might communicate differently.

6. How does the religion of Islam differ from Hinduism? Are there reasons beyond geographical location for grouping both religions under the rubric of "Eastern." What religion(s) are considered "Western?" How does this binary construction for dividing our world, cultures, religions, peoples, etc., frame our understanding of ourselves as "Westerners" and others as "Easterners"?

7. What is the influence of the American sense of "fair play" on decision making between German and American managers? If you were asked to help design a training program for a U.S. company that consistently engaged in business with Germany, what recommendations would you make after reading Friday's article?

Exercises

Exercise 2.1: Success Across Nations. This exercise ties into all the readings in Chapter 2 by having the students expand their definition of what it means to be successful. Having read about the values and culture of people from China, Korea, India, Africa, Egypt, and Germany it asks the students to do two things. First, it asks the students identify what success means to them. After evaluating their own definition of success, they will attempt to define what it means to be successful if you are a member of the 6 cultures examined in Chapter 2. So what is a successful Chinese, Korean, Indian, African, Egyptian, or German man? Woman? Child?

The second part of this exercise will give students experience interacting with people who may come from different cultural backgrounds than their own. As a basis of comparison between their own definition of success and the definitions of success based on the 6 cultures examined, ask the students to contact one to three people who did not grow up in the U.S. Students should interview each person and determine how each defines success and how each would describe themselves as a successful person. Some of the questions below will help students come up with their own definition, analyze the definitions of the 6 cultures, and conduct interviews with others:

Some questions for discussion.

1. How would you define a successful person?
2. How would you define the typical or "traditional" notion of a successful person?
3. Would you say that you are a successful person? Why or why not?

4. How does your success differ from the "traditional" notion of success?
5. How have the people in your life (family, friends, coworkers, spouse, etc.) influenced your success?
6. What problems have arisen for you in your work? What barriers have you had to overcome in order to be a successful person?
7. Have there been any problems relating or interacting with people that have influenced you negatively or positively as you became a successful person?
8. Has interacting with people from different countries and cultures had an impact on your success?

Ask students to write up their findings and compare them with other members of the class.

Exercise 2.2: Guest Speaker. This exercise encourages you to invite members of the Korean community into your classroom. Two options are suggested for this exercise.

Option 1: If you are in a community with a significant Korean and/or Korean American population, invite someone to come in and speak to the students about Robinson's article. It would be most productive to invite a business person who could speak to the relationship between intercultural communication and *nunch'i*.

Assign Robinson's article at least one class period ahead of the day the speaker is scheduled to come. Divide students into small groups and have them generate questions for the speaker. After the groups have generated a list of questions, have them choose their best two questions to turn in. Prepare a list of the students questions for the guest speaker so that he or she will have some idea of how class discussion might go. It might also be helpful to give the speaker a copy of your course syllabus so that he or she has a better understanding of the context within which the students are reading the Robinson article.

It is up to you and guest speaker to decide how the class will be run on the day he or she visits. One idea is to co-lead a discussion based on the questions prepared by the students. A second option is to give the speaker some time to lecture on *nunch'i* intercultural communication between Americans and Koreans, or Robinson's article, before leading a class discussion.

Option 2: Adapt option 1 into a series of short presentations of student-conducted interviews with Koreans/Korean Americans and/or short presentations by Korean American students about their experience and their family's experience with *nunch'i*.

Exercise 2.3: Values that Conflict and Correspond. This exercise can be used in conjunction with the Gannon article, "India: The Dance of Shiva". This activity asks the students to consider what they value in their life and make value comparisons between Indians as presented in the chapter, themselves, and a friend or acquaintance from a different cultural background. After reading the article, students can rank cultural values by using the value inventory scale on the next page. Students can use a scale of 1 (most valued) to 10 (least valued). After ranking the values for the Indian culture from the reading and ranking themselves, students are to ask a person from another country to rank the items.

Have the students report their findings to the class. Use the following questions to discuss students' responses. What were the five top values of the Indian culture? The top values that you ranked and the five top values of your friend? What differences and similarities are there? How do these rankings reflect the values of your cultures? What are some examples of how the Indian culture as well as you and your friend's culture have "taught" you to value certain things in life? What values, if any, were not on the list that you and/or your friend and/or a member of the Indian culture believe should have been included? How might differences in cultural values influence interpersonal interactions? How might such differences lead to interpersonal conflict? How much do similarities and differences in values enhance intercultural communication" What value differences might be insurmountable? Which would be incidental?

Exercise 2.3: Values that Conflict and Correspond

Value Inventory

Rank the following list of values from 1 (most valued) to 10 (least valued). Use Column A to record predicted Indian responses. Use Column B to record your responses. Then ask a person from another country to rank the items and record them in Column C. The definitions provided after each value are not meant to be definitive meanings. They are to allow you and your friend to complete this inventory using the same definitions for each value.

Value	A	B	C
1. Happiness (contentedness)	____	____	____
2. Freedom (independence, free choice)	____	____	____
3. Salvation (being saved, eternal life)	____	____	____
4. Family security (taking care of loved ones)	____	____	____
5. Self-respect (self-esteem)	____	____	____
6. Equality (sister- /brotherhood, equal opportunity)	____	____	____
7. Sense of accomplishment (making a lasting contribution)	____	____	____
8. A world at peace (free of war and international conflict)	____	____	____
9. Wisdom (a mature understanding of life)	____	____	____
10. A comfortable life (a prosperous life)	____	____	____

Value Comparison

Predicted Top Values of India	My Top Values	My Friend's Top Values
_____	_____	_____
_____	_____	_____
_____	_____	_____
_____	_____	_____
_____	_____	_____
_____	_____	_____
_____	_____	_____
_____	_____	_____
_____	_____	_____
_____	_____	_____

Exercise 2.4: Showing Our Emotions. In some cultures, the expression of anger by yelling and cursing may be acceptable. In others, it would be considered quite inappropriate. The extent to which we reveal ourselves through laughter, tears, anger, anxiousness, and jealousy depends in large part on how our families and communities displayed emotions and when we were chastised or rewarded as children for emoting inappropriately or appropriately. We learned from culture how to show and not show our feelings.

This exercise focuses on how often and intensely we show our emotions and how we feel when others express their emotions. This exercise is designed to help students understand more about their own emotional responses so that they might be in a better position to begin to understand how and why other cultures use emotion during interpersonal conversations.

Ask students to respond to the list of emotions provided as a handout on the next page by indicating from 1 to 6 how often they express these emotions and how comfortable they feel when others express them. Use the scales below to rate each emotion. The blank fine at the end of the list is for you or your students to fill in if you or they wish to add any emotions to the list.

After asking students to complete this list, ask them to consider the following questions. Which emotions do you have the least/most difficulty expressing and why? Which emotions do you have the least/most difficulty watching others express and why? Which discrepancies, if any, are there between the extent to which you are willing to show certain emotions and your feelings of comfort watching others express the same emotion? How do you think your expression of emotions and your responses to others' emotions have been influenced by cultural beliefs and attitudes? What differences and similarities are there in the displaying of emotions among your friends or classmates who come from different cultural backgrounds? How might intercultural communication be influenced by such differences?

between Raj and Tim have been alleviated? Think of what could have been done before, during, and after they met to prevent the breakdown of their friendship.

Test Items for Chapter 2

<u>Multiple Choice</u>

1.   Which of the following is a component of the Chinese face concept?
      a.   emotions
      b.   communication
      c.   identity
      d.   all of the above *

2.   Confucius classifies people into two kinds
      a.   junzi and xiao ren *
      b.   junzi and mianzi
      c.   junzi and lian
      d.   junzi and junz

3.   Which stage is the first most conscious moment for the transformation of the Chinese concept of face?
      a.   The formative stage
      b.   The mature stage
      c.   The Anti-Tradition stage *
      d.   The Communist Revolution stage

4.   During which stage does the face become separable from the human body and is treated as an object of central value?
      a.   The formative stage
      b.   The mature stage *
      c.   The Anti-Tradition stage
      d.   The Communist Revolution stage

5.   During which stage is *The Shi Ching*, a collection of folk poetry, discovered?
      a.   The formative stage *
      b.   The mature stage
      c.   The Anti-Tradition stage
      d.   The Communist Revolution stage

6. The slogan, "If you keep your face, you lose rice", is indicative of
   a. the formative stage
   b. the mature stage
   c. the Communist Revolution stage
   d. the Free Market Economy Stage *

7. The negative side of *nunch'i* refers to which of the following?
   a. deception with the goal of foreseeing
   b. deception with the goal of flattery
   c. deception with the goal of harmony *
   d. a & c

8. Pauses, silences, and rhetorical questions are examples of *nunch'i* acts that signal which of the following?
   a. support
   b. disagreement
   c. lack of understanding
   d. b & c *

9. Practicing *nunch'i* effectively requires which of the following qualities?
   a. sensitivity *
   b. logic
   c. sincerity
   d. clarity

10. A person who really understands *nunch'i* will focus on which of the following in a social interaction?
    a. expressing his/her desires to the other person in order to have them met
    b. understanding the desires of the other in order to express them
    c. predicting the other's desires in order to meet them *
    d. knowing his/her own desires in order to attain them

11. *Shiva* is known as
    a. The Creator
    b. The Preserver
    c. The Destroyer *
    d. None of the above

12. Action or activity is the definition of the Hindu term
    a. nirvana
    b. dharma
    c. karma *
    d. Brahman

13. According to Hinduism, the ultimate aim in life is to
    a. help those who remain in the lower levels of existence.
    b. remain pure of heart and soul.
    c. realize the most profound level of existence. *
    d. experience interconnectedness among all other Hindus.

14. Which of the following statements would people who follow raja yoga, the fourth Hindu path to salvation, be most likely to say?
    a. Love lies at the base of every heart.
    b. Work can be a vehicle for self-transcendence.
    c. Ignorance can be overcome through intense study.
    d. We must experience our bodies, our minds, and our spirits to their fullest potential. *

15. Which of the following statements would people who follow *karma yoga,* the third Hindu path to salvation, be most likely to say?
    a. Love lies at the base of every heart.
    b. Work can be a vehicle for self-transcendence. *
    c. Ignorance can be overcome through intense study.
    d. We must experience our bodies, our minds, and our spirits to their fullest potential.

16. According to Hindu Philosophy, during which stage of life is it the individual's prime responsibility to learn?
    a. Student *
    b. householder
    c. retirement
    d. all o f the above

17. Africa is made up of approximately
    a. 500 ethnic groups
    b. 1,000 ethnic groups
    c. 2,000 ethnic groups *
    d. 3,000 ethnic groups

18.   Which of the following is not the basic principle of the African culture?
      a.   unity
      b.   self-determination
      c.   individual work *
      d.   creativity

19.   Age grades consisted of segregated groups of males or females who were born
      a.   within a few years of each other*
      b.   the same year
      c.   ten years apart
      d.   none of the above

20.   Which of the following is NOT a central tenet of Islam?
      a.   There is only one God.
      b.   God created the world.
      c.   Humans must struggle to overcome their sinful nature.*
      e.   Every Muslim will go to heaven or hell.

21.   How old is Egyptian culture?
      a.   4-5000 years old *
      b.   2-3000 years old
      c.   7 centuries old
      d.   5 centuries old

22.   Which of the following is NOT fundamental to Egyptian culture?
      a.   tradition
      b.   relationships
      c.   hierarchical devotion
      d.   privacy *

23.   Which of the following does the Koran encourage?
      a.   Females who have reached puberty must cover themselves modestly.
      b.   Only women over the age of 20 must cover themselves.
      c.   Everyone must cover themselves modestly.
      e.   c, but especially a *

24.   Arabs have used the Arabic language to convey which of the following?
      a.   unity
      b.   worldview
      c.   artistic impressions
      d.   all of the above *

25. Muslims are required to stop for prayer
    a. once a day facing in the direction of the holy city of Mecca
    b. twice a day facing in the direction of the holy city of Mecca
    c. four times a day facing in the direction of the holy city of Mecca
    d. five times a day facing in the direction of the holy city of Mecca *

26. According to Friday, the American manager's expectation or need to be liked is in direct contrast with the German manager's need to be
    a. educated.
    b. credible. *
    c. confrontational.
    d. fair.

27. Unlike the German manager's orientation to his or her corporation, the American manager's orientation
    a. is long term.
    b. is typically formal.
    c. often consists of on-the-job training. *
    d. teaches specific rules and procedures.

28. One indication given by Friday that Germans tend to focus on the past more than their American counterparts is evidenced in the fact that
    a. German architecture is older than American architecture.
    b. Americans engaged in space exploration before the Germans.
    c. Germans tend to begin discussions with historical background information.*
    d. Americans have lower standards for higher education than their German counterparts.

True/False

T   1. Communication is a fundamental part of face.
T   2. Face is not a static concept but a dynamic and fluid one.
F   3. Self to the Chinese resides in the face.
F   4. Because of *nunch'i*, Koreans are not very concerned with what others see in and think about them.
F   5. *Nunch'i* might not exist if Korea had a hierarchical social system.
T   6. The use of *nunch'i* requires self-control.
T   7. *Nunch'i* figuring-out is a response to *nunch'i* execution.
T   8. Among Hindus, dancing is regarded as the most ancient and important of the arts.
T   9. Shiva is a diety that dances simply as an expression of his exuberant personality.
T   10. According to Hindu philosophy, a person can pass through the four stages of life in a single lifetime or stay at each stage for many lifetimes.

T	11.	In India the lower down the economic hierarchy the more equal are the relations between the sexes.
T	12.	Belief in witchcraft and magical powers is widespread across the continent of Africa.
F	13.	Most cultures in Africa are based on individualism.
T	14.	Four tenets are central to understanding Islam.
T	15.	Islam possesses a universal allure, which appeals to Egyptians.
T	16.	Good Muslims follow the five pillars.
T	17.	When Germans and Americans come together in discussion, the Germans' drive is to establish hierarchy, the American's is to dissolve it.
T	18.	According to Friday, American managers approach the business relationship more impersonally than German managers.
F	19.	German managers are more likely to be selected and promoted based on personal accomplishments than their education and credentials.
F	20	Traditionally, German managers share the American sense of "fair play."
T	21.	American managers being trained to work with their German counterparts will best learn through interactive role plays when the focus is on debriefing the informal rules of the interaction.

Essay Questions

1. Explain how communication is a fundamental part of face.
2. According to Emmanuel Levinas, "Face and discourse are tied. The face speaks. It speaks, it is in this that it renders possible and begins all discourse". Describe this phenomenon.
3. Explain the statement, "The fewer written legal codes that people create for regulating a people's interaction, the more significant the unwritten concept of face becomes in such a community."
4. Identify five stages of transformation the Chinese concept has experienced and briefly review each stage.
5. Explain the three assumptions Carbaugh makes about communication.
6. Why wouldn't such North American practices as "Dutch treat" be seen favorably by Koreans?
7. Why are face-saving and "anticipatory communication" such important parts of East Asian communication?
8. Describe *nunch'i* and compare it to a Euro-American communcative style or sensibility.
9. Discuss the relationship between *nunch'i* and hierarchical social relations in Korea.
10. What does the Dance of Shiva symbolize?
11. Discuss how the Dance of Shiva relates to Hindu Philosophy.
12. Explain the four stages of life that an individual passes through, according to Hindu Philosophy.
13. Describe the different facets or types of *dharma* that guide a person through his or her life.
14. How does the caste system in India influence communication among its people?
15. Describe the Hindu concept of Karma.

Instructor's Resource Manual

for

Samovar and Porter's

Intercultural Communication:
A Reader

Tenth Edition

Donna Gotch
California State University, San Bernardino

THOMSON

WADSWORTH

Australia • Canada • Mexico • Singapore • Spain • United Kingdom • United States

Printed in the United States of America
1 2 3 4 5 6 7 06 05 04 03

Printer: Victor Graphics, Inc.

ISBN: 0-534-56497-6

For more information about our products,
contact us at:
Thomson Learning Academic Resource Center
1-800-423-0563

For permission to use material from this text,
contact us by:
Phone: 1-800-730-2214
Fax: 1-800-731-2215
Web: http://www.thomsonrights.com

Wadsworth/Thomson Learning
10 Davis Drive
Belmont, CA 94002-3098
USA

Asia
Thomson Learning
5 Shenton Way #01-01
UIC Building
Singapore 068808

Australia
Nelson Thomson Learning
102 Dodds Street
South Street
South Melbourne, Victoria 3205
Australia

Canada
Nelson Thomson Learning
1120 Birchmount Road
Toronto, Ontario M1K 5G4
Canada

Europe/Middle East/South Africa
Thomson Learning
High Holborn House
50/51 Bedford Row
London WC1R 4LR
United Kingdom

Latin America
Thomson Learning
Seneca, 53
Colonia Polanco
11560 Mexico D.F.
Mexico

Spain
Paraninfo Thomson Learning
Calle/Magallanes, 25
28015 Madrid, Spain

16. Discuss the Indian proverb, "A son should be treated as a prince for five years; as a slave for ten years; but from his sixteenth birthday, as a friend."

17. Discuss the role of women in the Indian culture.

18. Identify and review the four tenets which are central to understanding Islam.

19. Explain the importance of tradition to Egyptian culture.

20. Why is the religion of Islam considered a religion of practices? What are the five pillars **outlined** for Muslims by the religion of Islam? What does each suggest about Islamic values?

21. What attitude do Egyptians usually take to the hierarchical structure of their society? What does the religion of Islam say about hierarchical social positions? Could these be examples of how cultures tend to be self-justifying? Consider Protestantism and the American call to "pull yourself up by your own bootstraps."

22. Explain the connection between language and cultural unity using the example of Arabic in 7th century Egyptian society.

23. Explain the importance of relationships to Egyptian culture.

24. Explain the idea of *Insha'allah* ("If God wills it") as part of Muslim beliefs.

25. After reading the articles in Chapter 2, can you describe an Eastern way of communicating and a Western way of communicating?

26. Compare and contrast the German and American manager's focus with regard to their orientation to cooperation and relationship to business.

27. Indicate how differences in education, learning styles, and problem solving between German and American managers may influence their learning styles.

28. What does Friday mean by the term "guidance system" and of what importance is it to his discussion of German and American managers?

29. Define the German term *Besprechung.*

30. What difference might it make that American managers are more oriented toward the future than German managers who are grounded in their past tradition?

31. If you were asked to help design a training program for a U.S. company that consistently engaged in business with Germany, what recommendations would you make after reading Friday's article?

Chapter References

Artman, R. (1976). The Miami Intercultural Communication Workshop. In David S. Hoopes (Ed.), <u>Readings in Intercultural Communication: Vol. V--Intercultural Programming</u> (pp. 68-106). Pittsburgh, PA: The Intercultural Communication Network.

Feig, J. P., and Blair, J. G. (1975). <u>There IS a Difference: Seventeen Intercultural Perspectives</u>, Washington, DC: Meridian House International.

Chapter 3
Co-Cultures: Living in Two Cultures

Chapter Synopsis

This chapter examines the cultural patterns that influence the communication of certain cultural groups in the United States. Five distinct questions form the foundation of this chapter: (1) What does it mean and feel like to be the *other in* U.S. society? (2) How do power, dominance, and nondominance manifest themselves in intracultural U.S. communication? (3) What are some cultural characteristics of nondominant cultures in the U.S. and how do these differ from those of "mainstream" U.S. culture? (4) How do members of these cultures communicate intra- and interculturally? (5) With what challenges must members of these U.S. cultures contend as they live and communicate in the U.S.?

Kim reveals four types of interethnic communication messages; assimiliationism, pluralism, reconciliation, and extremism. Examples are provided for each type of message. Jackson and Dangerfield examine Black Masculinity and the factors that affect masculine positioning. An overview is provided of three prominent social and racial stereotypes of Black masculinities. Garrett and Wilbur explore some of the basic cultural elements contributing to what is known as Native American spirituality. Four concepts which are central to the Native American spirituality are discussed: Medicine, Relation, Harmony, and Vision.

Bronski provides insight into the Gay culture. He provides a historical overview of the gay culture and explains that there is no single "gay identity". Bronski describes many characteristics of the gay culture and provides an understanding of the elements of the gay culture. Wood and Reich clearly explain the difference between sex and gender. They posit that sex is genetically determined whereas gender is socially constructed. They discuss boy's and girl's games and how children play at these games is result in two very different styles of communicating. They provide six ways communication between males and females might be improved.

Braithwaite and Braithwaite use the comments of persons with disabilities to describe their experiences communicating with members of the "temporarily able-bodied" community. Students will receive valuable information not just about persons with disabilities but actually from persons with disabilities. McKay illustrates through research literature and example, the characteristics of the co-culture of the elderly. This article will help students understand the complex and interesting lives that many elderly people lead. In addition, negative myths and stereotypes are dispelled and the special relationship between grandparents and grandchildren is explored.

Discussion Ideas

1. Ask students to engage in a class discussion on the following Orwellian quote: "All men are created equal--some are just more equal than others."
    a. Begin by inviting students to look closely at the terms in the sentence. Who is not included? What does "equal" mean? What does it mean to be "created equal"?
    b. Next, ask students to consider U.S. society. Who are the "some" that are more equal in the United States? Why are these people more equal than others9 What do they have, what privileges do they have, that others don't? Who are those that are not "as equal" as those who are "more equal"? What prevents them from being as equal as the others? Use Folb's article to remind students of the historical construction of power, dominance, and nondominance in the U.S.
    c. Finally, ask students why, if we know that some people are more equal than others, does this situation persist in society today" Why hasn't it been changed? What will have to happen to make all people equal to each others Is this possible? Are hierarchically structured, classist societies inevitable? Will there always be those on the bottom and those on top?

2. How is black masculinity portrayed by the media? Discuss some of the stereotypical ways which Black males are portrayed in television, film, magazines, etc. What can be done to promote more positive Black roles for men? How can the media assist in this promotion?

3. How is gender a social phenomenon? Do you agree with Wood and Reich that our gender is the product of socialization? Or is it primarily, or at least partially, a biological phenomenon? Do you think male/female relations can be improved using the strategies that Wood and Reich suggests?

4. Prior to reading the McKay article, were you aware that many elderly people lead complex and interesting lives? Do you know elderly people who do? Did you have or do you have a special relationship with a grandparent or both grandparents as described by McKay? Did/does this relationship help you view other elderly people in a different light rather than via typical stereotypes?

5. Why are nondisabled persons often so uncomfortable interacting with persons with disabilities?
    a. Ask students to consider this question by reflecting on their own experiences communicating with persons with disabilities. What made them uncomfortable? What was different about communicating with the person with a disability from communicating with nondisabled persons?

b. Discuss the prevalence of uncertainty and unfamiliarity in intercultural communication. These feelings are very common and often account for much of our discomfort during intercultural interactions. What is often unfamiliar about communicating with persons with disabilities? What might we be uncertain about when we communicate with persons with disabilities?

c. Using Braithwaite's suggestions as supporting material, ask students how they can go about becoming more comfortable with communication between themselves and persons with disabilities. What can they do? How can they view the other persons

6. Thinking back on all of the articles in the chapter, do you think it is a privilege to live in only one culture or a privilege to inhabit multiple cultures? Why or why not? (You may want to record student responses on the board for the questions below.) What about the power differential between the elderly and the young/middle aged as compared to the differential between gay and straight individuals in our society? How does power act differently to favor one and discriminate against the other in each of these groupings? Give concrete examples.

Exercises

Exercise 3.1: Political Correctness or Necessary Changes? This exercise incorporates themes from all the articles in chapter 3. It asks students to consider the popular phrase "political correctness" and determine for themselves whether it is a movement that suppresses free speech or whether it is, in part, really about changes in our language and perception of other cultures. Changes in how we talk about and refer to people often influence how we perceive those people. Take the evolution of the word *crippled* to refer to those individuals who use wheelchairs and walk with the aid of crutches. Over the past few decades, the word *crippled* went from *handicapped* to *disabled* to *physically challenged*. If you look at the progression of these terms and the more tolerant and inclusive social and legal changes that have affected physically challenged individuals, you can see a gradual positive development in how members of this group perceive themselves and are perceived by the able-bodied members of society. The same type of language evolution can be found in terms regarding African Americans, women, gays and lesbians, and the elderly. As our language changes, attitudes and policies sometimes change with it. Although there may not be a direct causal fink between language changes and policy and attitude changes, it is clear that language shapes our perception of the world and its people in different ways. With changes in perception come changes in how we act toward and interact with people. Guadalupe Friaz, assistant professor of ethnic studies at the University of Washington, describes language as political and always changing.

When we talk about language we're talking about the relationships between people, and what people call each other reflects whatever tension and anxiety that society is going through.... Change is constant.... Group relationships always change, so of course terminology is going to change. (de Leon & Macdonald, 1992, p. A1)

Change inevitably brings about many different kinds of tension and disagreement in a society. Decisions must be made about whether to make changes, how to go about making changes, who will make the changes, who will be affected, etc. Changes in our language, school curricula, and teaching strategies are just a few examples of the transitions taking place in the United States today as a result of a heightened awareness of diversity.

The term "political correctness" is often used to describe this increased awareness and shift toward more inclusive and specific language. Those who have coined the phrase "political correctness" feel that these changes in language and thought have bred a climate of intolerance on university campuses. Some people have perceived enormous pressure to use the *right* terms when talking about certain cultural groups. Others even feel that their freedom of speech has been suppressed when they are chastised for espousing views that are not in step with the current climate of multiculturalism and diversity.

Engage students in a dialogue about "political correctness" and what it means to them. We would suggest that you have students discuss several of the questions below in small groups and then have each group report out the results of their discussion. You may also wish to have students write on the general question, "What is political correctness?" the day before having a class discussion. This kind of exercise can turn into a very spirited and even emotional debate on the merits and disadvantages of "political correctness." Encourage students to be honest about their own opinions yet respectful of their classmates' opinions as well.

Some questions to consider in small groups and as a larger class:

1. List some earlier terms used to identify African Americans, women, gays, lesbians, and the elderly. Then list the more recent politically correct terms.
2. Define what you think the phrase "political correctness" means.
3. Offer an alternative definition of "political correctness," perhaps an opposing view from your own.
4. Why have there been such negative opinions expressed in the media about political correctness? What's wrong with advocating and using "politically correct" language?
5. What do you think about the linguistic and social changes that are currently taking place in our society?
6. Do you feel that there is pressure to be "politically correct"? Or is being "politically correct" really just about being sensitive to and respectful of all members of U.S. society?
7. What is there to be gained in our society by using language that refers more precisely to the cultural backgrounds of individuals? Conversely, what are the problems with using exact terms to refer to different groups of people?
8. Consider this scenario. You are participating in a classroom discussion and use the word *black* to refer to U. S. citizens of African ancestry. A person in the class

corrects you and explains that *African American* is the preferred term. What is your reaction to this correction?

9.   How can we know how to refer to and address members of certain cultural groups?

10.   Does it really matter what we call people? Can those people who are U.S. citizens just be called simply "Americans"? Why or why not?

Exercise 3.2: Privilege in U.S. Society. This exercise asks students to examine U. S. society and determine which groups enjoy certain privileges to which many other groups do not have access. It is common among those who have the "room at the top" to assume that other individuals have equal access to society's opportunities, rights, and services, not realizing that people's personal worlds are made up of experiences that can be very culture-specific and biased against other groups. The assumption that people are the same and share the same societal benefits can strain and even hinder the development of intercultural relationships because such an assumption is based on a lack of awareness and sensitivity to an acquaintance, friend, or romantic partner's experiences. By examining the societal privileges that
several groups enjoy, we can increase the awareness of and sensitivity to others' experiences that can be so crucial in intercultural communication.

One way to introduce this exercise on privilege in U.S. society to students is to begin with an example of Euro-American privilege. "White privilege" is a phrase used to identify advantages that many European Americans have that are often not available to people of color. A serious and disturbing example of white privilege is the tendency for African American men to be stopped for questioning by the police in upscale neighborhoods where they may be perceived as suspicious or "out of place." Euro-American males usually do not suffer this kind of discrimination under these same circumstances. While some groups may enjoy more privileges than others, all groups have greater access to certain privileges than others. For example, women, in general, are probably stopped by police for questioning less frequently than men. Thus we might say that white males more so than black males, and women more so than men, have greater access to the "privilege" of not being unnecessarily harassed by the police.

The questions below focus on issues of privilege and culture. Some will be very difficult for students because they will require information regarding cultural groups about which they may know very little. Most likely, the more diverse your class is, the more varied and informative will be the discussion. Ask students to consider many of the different cultural characteristics of U.S. society when answering the questions. For example, laws, societal norms, traditions, stereotypes, prejudices, etc. Students should first discuss these questions in small groups. Afterward engage the class in a discussion by having each group report on its responses. Watch for assumptions being made as the discussion progresses. That is, are statements being made that assume students' experiences and perceptions are shared by other U.S. residents?

You may wish to give different questions to different groups so that all questions are covered. Add other questions not listed here and ask students to generate their own questions.

Questions

1. What societal privileges do you think European Americans have greater access to than other cultural groups? Are there any privileges that non-European Americans have that European Americans do not?
2. What societal privileges do you think heterosexuals enjoy that gay men and women do not?
3. What societal privileges do men enjoy that women do not?
4. What societal privileges do women enjoy that men do not?
5. What societal privileges do able-bodied individuals enjoy that disabled individuals do not?
6. What societal privileges do same-race couples enjoy that different race couples do not?
7. What societal privileges do opposite-sex couples enjoy that same sex couples do not?

Exercise 3.3: Exploring Racial Relations. It asks students to reflect on communication effectiveness, communication issues, and communication improvement strategies identified in the article. Students are to examine a recent media issue involving European Americans and African Americans. For example, the demonstrations and riots that took place after the "not guilty" verdicts were announced in the Rodney King police brutality trial, affirmative action issues, the O. J. Simpson trial, etc. Have the students analyze the effectiveness of the communication surrounding the event by determining if the seven primary issues of importance (negative stereotyping, acceptance, personal expressiveness, authenticity, understanding, goal attainment, and power dynamics) to African Americans were addressed/acknowledged/met, as well as issues of importance to European Americans.

Questions

1. Were any of the identified communication improvement strategies used? If so, what were they? How effective were they? If not, would the situation have improved if they were used?
2. How can both European Americans and African Americans work together to improve their interaction?
3. Are these solutions possible on an institutional level as well as on a personal level?
4. What are some of your own solutions for improving interaction between European Americans and African Americans?

Exercise 3.4: Visible and Invisible Cultural Markers. This exercise is designed to be used with Bronski's article. It should help students to think about gay male culture in relation to the other co-cultures discussed in Chapter 3. Divide the class into six groups. Assign each group one of the following cultural markers: race, religion, sexual orientation, gender, age, and economic class. Ask students to answer the questions listed below in terms of their group's assigned cultural identity marker. Remind students to back up their responses with specific, concrete examples.

1. What makes race, religion, sexual orientation, gender, age, or economic class a culture?
2. Can a person mark or display an affiliation with this culture? How might they do this?
3. Is it optional or mandatory for a person who belongs to this culture to wear their membership?
4. How might the distinction between optional and mandatory cultural markers relate back to class discussions about privilege in U.S. society?
5. Are individuals penalized more for belonging to certain non-mainstream cultures as opposed to others? Why?

Have each group share their responses with the class and then lead an all-class discussion using some of the following questions. What is culture? Do you have to see it for it to be a culture? Do outsiders have to recognize a culture in order for it to be legitimate? What are some possible effects of including this information in a college textbook? How is this similar to the practice of "outing" members of the gay community? What happens when you make visible formerly invisible practices/norms of subcultures? What is at stake, what are the risks to the subculture?

Exercise 3.5: Sexual Harassment or Friendly Behavior? Sexual harassment in professional environments has become a major and controversial issue in the past few years. It is an issue that has raised the consciousness of employers and employees, professors and students, and men and women in general. Sexual harassment is about many things: the abuse of power over subordinates and women, the definition of appropriate conduct in a working environment, and the right of all individuals to work in a nonthreatening, noncoercive setting. At a more basic level, however, sexual harassment is often about how the same behavior can be perceived quite differently by the people involved. This exercise focuses on mate/female differences in behavior perception and can be used in conjunction with the Wood and Reich article.

This case study asks students to consider the role of perception in sexual harassment. Why do men and women often perceive the same behavior quite differently? How do men define "appropriate behavior" in the workplace? How do women define it? Before asking students to read and discuss the case study below in small groups, have them answer the first question about sexual harassment. Choose from among questions two through ten for students to answer with their group members; ask students to consider the remaining questions as a large class. Although this is a topic that lends itself to a great deal of debate and even conflict, encourage students to be as honest in their responses as possible.

Case Study on Sexual Harassment

1. How would you define sexual harassment? (Please don't give a legal definition. Draw from your own opinions and experiences.) Now read the case study below and consider the questions that follow.

   Susan worked as a welder for a small, privately owned auto parts manufacturer. After only a few weeks on the job, she began to notice that centerfold pin-ups from men's magazines were prominently displayed at individual work sites around the shop. There were also pictures of nude women tacked to the company's community bulletin board. Susan asked her only female colleague, Joan, why these pictures were there but Joan just shrugged her shoulders and said, "I guess because they like to look at them while they're working." Joan seemed unconcerned about the pictures.

   But the pictures really bothered, even offended Susan. Susan felt that the pictures were pornographic and had no place in a work setting. She had to look at them whenever she went to talk to another employee or even pass their work stations, and she could not read the bulletin board without seeing the pictures there. After talking with her supervisor about her concern, he agreed to take down the pictures on the bulletin board but said that the men had a right to display the pictures at their individual work stations because that was their private space. Susan then asked individuals if they would display their centerfold pictures in less conspicuous places. All refused and said to "mellow out" because she was taking the issue too seriously. They felt the pictures were tasteful and anyway, "naked women are beautiful," they explained.

   Susan was not convinced. She continued to ask her supervisor for help but, getting nowhere, went to the director of the company. He also did nothing. Meanwhile, it appeared that even more pictures were being put up in plain sight of Susan's work station. While a few men did understand her outrage, they did not join her in her struggle to eliminate the pictures. Frustrated with the situation. she quit her job after only six months.

2. Compare your definitions of sexual harassment. Are there differences among group members?

3. Based on your definitions, was Susan experiencing sexual harassment? Why or why not?

4. How did most of Susan's coworkers and her supervisor perceive the display of centerfold pictures?

5. Why was Susan reacting so strongly to these displays?

6. Whose perceptions of this situation do you support (if anyone's) in this case study? Explain your answer.

7. Do you feel that Susan's coworkers had a right to display pictures of nude women at their own work stations? Explain your answer.

8. What rights did Susan have as an employee of the company.?

9. Given each of your answers above, how would you have resolved this controversy if you had been Susan? A fellow coworker? Her supervisor? Director of the company.? Have one group member take on the role of one of these people and be prepared to report to the class their individual perspectives.

10. Do you think that women and men perceive sexual harassment differently? If so, how can such differences be resolved in the work place? Were there differences among your group members? If so, were these differences along gender lines?

Exercise 3.6: Trading Places. This exercise is to be used in conjunction with the Wood and Reich article "Gendered Speech Communities". Ask each student to consider the following scenario and answer the following questions.

Imagine if you were to wake up tomorrow morning as a member of the opposite sex. Think about what that would be like. Answer the following questions anonymously on paper.

1. What would be different about your life?
2. What would be better about your life?
3. What would be worse about your life?

After all students have completed writing their responses, collect them and begin to read responses aloud. The responses written by both and men and women can be very insightful and provide valuable material for discussion. Some typical responses by males if they were to wake up as a female include: "I would have to spend more time on my physical appearance", and "I wouldn't walk alone late at night". Some typical responses by females if they were to wake up as a male include: "I would be more respected at work", and "I could use more profanity when speaking to friends". This exercise generates a lot of discussion and serves as a good supplement to the article about gender.

Exercise 3.7: My Elder, My Friend. This exercise is associated with the McKay article "Communication Dynamics of the Elderly" and sends students into the "field" to actually experience this co-culture. The objective is to make the students aware of the complex and interesting lives led by many elderly and to encourage intergenerational relationships. Students may work alone or in groups on this assignment. They are to spend one hour with an interesting person whom they consider elderly. This person can be a relative, professor, acquaintance, etc. students should interview the person asking some of the following questions as well as any questions they would like to add. Students will then report their findings to the class.

1.   Do you work or are you retired? Are you enjoying work/retirement?

2.   What did you do that was particularly enjoyable this week?

3.   Who are your closest friends? How often do you see them?

4.   What are your hobbies?

5.   Where did you go on your last trip?

6.   Do you vote?

7.   Do you have grandchildren? How often do you see them?

8.   Do you feel that younger people don't understand you?

9.   What things have you done in your life that you would change if you could?

10.   What things have you done in your life that you are particularly proud of?

11.   What is your favorite personal story?

12.   What advice would you give to college students?

Exercise 3.8: Interactions Among the Disabled and Ablebodied. It is not uncommon for some people to feel uncomfortable around physically challenged individuals. Braithwaite & Braithwaite describes in their article the kind of communication that often occurs when an ablebodied and physically challenged person interact: greater physical distance, less eye contact, and shorter duration of talk. It is common for ablebodied, or "temporarily ablebodied," persons to focus on the disability instead of the person when interacting with disabled individuals. As a result, ablebodied individuals may be unsure of how to interact with less ablebodied people, and wonder nervously to themselves, "What can I say to this person *with a disability?*" They might do better to simply ask themselves, "What can I share with this person?"

Another feeling of uncertainty that might arise for an ablebodied person is how much assistance should they offer, or should they wait until a physically challenged person asks for assistance. When hearing people interact with members of the deaf culture, Jankowski (1991) says it is common for hearing people to believe that "they can explain things better because of the 'communication barrier' and will proceed with the conversation as though the deaf person were not there" (p. 149).

This exercise asks ablebodied students to consider their own feelings about and communicative behavior during interactions with disabled individuals. Ask students to read the following "Dear Abby" letter and answer the questions that follow in a small group. As with many of the exercises given in this manual this exercise may be most effectively conducted by first having students consider in writing their perceptions of the disabled. Each group should have an opportunity to report their small group discussion findings in the larger class discussion.

Dear Abby:

You have championed many causes for the physically challenged, and I thank you for all you have done. Now, will you please do us one more favor? Please advise waiters, waitresses, flight attendants, and everyone else who serves the public, of the following:

Because a person happens to be in a wheelchair with leg braces--or appears to be partially paralyzed due to polio, cerebral palsy, a stroke, or some unknown cause-please do not assume that he of she can neither think nor speak. I was badly clobbered by polio many years ago, but have been rehabilitated greatly, thanks to physical therapy, my own determination and a lot of hard work. However, I am in a wheelchair and somewhat physically impaired. When I am in a restaurant (or on a plane) and food orders are being taken, please speak directly to me. Do not turn to my companion and ask, "And what will SHE have?"

CAN COMMUNICATE IN MARIETTA, OHIO (Dear Abby, 1993, p. 8)

Some questions for discussion: Why do people often communicate with disabled persons in the manner described by "Can Communicate in Marietta"? What messages do they send to the disabled person when they communicate in this way? Have you ever felt uncomfortable communicating with someone who was in a wheelchair or in some way physically disabled or challenged? Why do you think you felt this way? What kept or keeps you from communicating, if at all, with a person who is disabled? Describe your last communication encounter with a disabled person. How can you break the communication barriers between you and a disabled person?

Test Items for Chapter 3

Multiple Choice

1.   "Melting pot" and "color blind society" are metaphors for which of the following interethnic communication message
      a.   assimilationism *
      b.   pluralism
      c.   reconciliation
      d.   extremism

2. The idea of sanctity of the group is a message of
   a. assimilationism
   b. pluralism *
   c. reconciliation
   d. extremism

3. Alan Wolfe (1998) describes the "vital center" – the "middle" America as being the voices of
   a. assimiliationism
   b. pluralism
   c. reconciliation *
   d. extremism

4. Those messages which express a preference for a maximum in-group-out-group separation are messages of
   a. assimiliationism
   b. pluralism
   c. reconciliation
   d. extremism *

5. The messages of reconciliation reflect the struggle of Americans seeking which of the following?
   a. moderation *
   b. flexibility
   c. separation
   d. none of the above

6. Messages from the The New Black Panthers and the Nation of Islam's are those of
   a. extremism *
   b. moderation
   c. pluralism
   d. reconciliation

7. The popular phrases in the Black community "Stay black" and "Keep it real" are statements of the Black masculine positionality of
   a. struggle
   b. community
   c. achievement *
   d. independence

8. The entire concept of masculinity is predicated on which of the following?
   a. struggle
   b. community
   c. achievement
   d. recognition *

9. The use of rigid racial categories that distort an African American's individuality is called
   a. bigotry
   b. negative stereotyping *
   c. labeling
   d. contexting

10. Which of the following social projections about the Black masculine body comply with public narratives which pertain to Black men's lives?
    a. violent
    b. sexual
    c. incompetent
    d. all of the above *

11. Which popular toy store received complaints from consumers for promoting stereotypes that were gender specific?
    a. FAO Schwartz
    b. Toys 'R Us *
    c. Boy's World
    e. Girl's World

12. Which of the following is not considered a Native American belief?
    a. There is a single higher power known as Creator
    b. The spirit world exists side by side with the physical world
    c. The spirit will no longer be a part of the body after the body dies *
    d. Illness affects the mind and spirit as well as the body

13. Which of the following four concepts to Native American spirituality emphasizes understanding the direction to one's path as a caretaker?
    a. Medicine
    b. Relation
    c. Vision *
    d. Harmony

14. Which of the following four concepts to Native American spirituality emphasizes the Circle of Life?
    a. Medicine
    b. Relation *
    c. Vision
    d. Harmony

15. Which of the following four concepts to Native American spirituality emphasizes acceptance?
    a. Medicine
    b. Relation
    c. Harmony *
    d. Vision

16. The "velvet mafia" refers to
    a. a gay network of influential men in the entertainment industry *
    b. gay men who wear red scarfs
    c. hetereosexual theater critics
    d. none of the above

17. Which of the following are coded as representations of the gay experience?
    a. the works of Tennessee Williams
    b. the writings of Gertrude Stein
    c. the plays of Oscar Wilde
    d. all of the above *

18. What is the cultural meaning of sex?
    a. sexuality
    b. gender*
    c. sexual orientation
    d. eroticism

19. A set of norms regarding how to communicate that is shared by a group of people is called a communication
    a. collective
    b. community
    c. culture *
    d. grouping

20. What are the two primary influences on gender socialization?
   a. school and family
   b. media and school
   c. intimate and platonic relationships
   d. family dynamics and peer interaction *

21. When compared to boys' games, girls' games tend to include fewer people and rules are relatively
   a. ambiguous and unimportant
   b. numerous and complex
   c. set and rigid
   d. unfixed and negotiated *

22. Wood and Reich suggests that feedback and response cues such as "uh huh" and "hmm" from women can indicate which of the following to men?
   a. agreement *
   b. condescension
   c. desire
   d. weakness

23. Which of the following is NOT a severe consequence of stereotyping?
   a. The stereotyped group may engage in self-fulfilling behavior.
   b. Those who have preconceived notions may act upon their beliefs.
   c. The self-esteem and self confidence of the stereotyped group may suffer.
   d. Interactions may improve only in a general sense. *

24. According to McKay, the positive stereotype someone who is "retired, conservative, old-fashioned, nostalgic, and religious is known as
   a. the "Golden Ager"
   b. the "John Wayne Conservative *
   c. the "Small Town Neighbor"
   d. the "Perfect Grandparents"

25. According to McKay, the "Golden Ager" is described as
   a. active, adventurous, healthy, wealthy, and interesting. *
   b. retired, conservative, and old-fashioned.
   c. political and liberal.
   d. old and frumpy.

26. According to McKay, the "Elitist" is
    a.   greedy, miserly, snobbish, emotionless, and humorous
    b.   demanding, prejudiced, and wary *
    c.   tired, frustrated, worried, and lonely
    d.   quiet, timid, dependent, forgetful, and naïve

27. The elderly can be identified as co-culture because
    a.   they are distinguished from the larger culture. *
    b.   they are a homogeneous group.
    c.   they have many contributions to society.
    a.   None of these answers are true.

28. For older adults, friendships revolve around which of the following?
    a.   a sense of community
    b.   help
    c.   transportation
    d.   all of the above *

29. One intergenerational relationship that seem to transcend the negative stereotypes of aging is the relationship between
    a.   parents and children.
    b.   grandparents and grandchildren. *
    c.   siblings with younger siblings.
    d.   All of the above.

30. McKay feels that there is as much diversity within the elderly population as between it and any other group because
    a.   the elderly have seen dramatic technological advances in their lifetime.
    b.   they usually have had long-term marriages.
    c.   they have lived through at least one war.
    d.   all of the above. *

31. How many people in the U.S. have some type of disability?
    a.   one in five people *
    b.   one in ten people
    c.   one in twenty people
    d.   one in thirty people

32. Which of the following was identified by Crewe and Athelstan (1985) as a "key life function" that may be affected by a disability?
    a. mobility
    b. employment
    c. self-care
    d. all of the above *

33. Which of the following forms of redefinition by the disabled describes the following comment made by one of Braithwaite's informants: "I am a person like anyone else."
    a. redefinition as members of a new culture
    b. redefinition of self *
    c. redefinition of disability
    d. redefinition of life

34. Viewing a disability as a characteristic of a person rather than the person her or himself recognizes disability as
    a. inherent.
    b. inevitable.
    c. situational. *
    d. occupational.

35. The label "handicapped person" is problematic and objectionable to people with disabilities because it emphasizes the disability instead of the
    a. culture
    b. relationship
    c. situation
    d. person *

36. Nonhandicapped or nondisabled persons are often referred to as _____ by members of the disabled culture.
    a. temporarily able-bodied *
    b. normal
    c. ablebodied
    d. futurely disabled

37. Of the three phases identified when adjusting to a disability which includes an individuals focus on rehabilitation and all of the physical changes they are experiencing?
    a. stigma isolation *
    b. stigma recognition
    c. stigma incorporation
    d. stigma denial

38. Of the three phases identified when adjusting to a disability which phase is identified as one where the individual has not yet noticed the changes in their social relationships or communication with nondisabled others?
   a. stigma isolation *
   b. stigma recognition
   c. stigma incorporation
   d. stigma denial

True/False

T	1.	Messages expressed by Skinheads as well as Louis Farrakhan are considered messages of extremism.
T	2.	When "Ebonics" was endorsed by the Oakland Unified School District many public leaders denounced it as being "extremist".
T	3.	The ideological circle encompasses the four ideological postions.
F	4.	Masculinity is natural and innate.
T	5.	Masculinity is learned.
F	6.	Some definitions of Masculinity are a matter of positionality.
F	7.	Native Americans have been able to legally practice their spirituality and traditional ways in this country since 1968 when the American Indian Religious Freedom Act passed.
T	8.	According to Native American beliefs illness affects the mind, body and spirit.
T	9.	According to Native American beliefs there is medicine in every event, memory place, person, and movement.
F	10.	According to Native American beliefs there are "good experiences" and "bad experiences" in life.
T	11.	According to Native American beliefs the spirit world exists side by side with the physical world.
F	12.	Native Americans believe that the spirit exited in the spirit world after it lives the physical body.
T	13.	A great deal of gay male culture has been centered on the creation, cultivation, and appreciation of the arts.
T	14.	The character of the West African trickster in slave culture has a gay corollary.
T	15.	One reason why Gay Culture was able to maintain its protective status is that it did not conform to the traditional definitions of a subculture
T	16.	Gay culture is placed distinctly outside the family networks that nurture most other subcultures.
F	17.	We are born with a gender.
T	18.	Gender is socially constructed.
F	19.	Gender and sex are synonymous.
T	20.	We may choose to embody different genders in different situations.
T	21.	No person is born with a particular gender.
T	22.	Girls and boys tend to define self in different ways.

T	23.	Senior citizens are as unique and diverse as most members of the younger population in our society.
F	24.	When using stereotypes as a form of categorization, individual differences are taken into account.
T	25.	Negative stereotypes of the elderly are created by young people, middle age people, and the elderly alike.
F	26.	Research indicates that intergenerational relationships rarely serve a productive function for either party.
F	27.	The nonverbal communication of an able-bodied person usually signals acceptance more so than the verbal message.
T	28.	Disability affects the behavioral, economic, and social aspects of a person's life.

Essay Questions

1. Discuss assimilationist messages. Provide examples of these types of messages in your response.
2. Discuss pluralist messages. Provide examples of these types of messages in your response.
3. Discuss reconciliation messages. Provide examples of these types of messages in your response.
4. Discuss messages of extremism. Provide examples of these types of messages in your response.
5. Differentiate between messages of pluralism and messages of assimilation.
6. Explain the *ideological circle*.
7. Briefly overview the three prominent social and racial stereotypes of Black masculinities.
8. Differentiate between male and female sex and gender role stereotypes.
9. Discuss the four concepts that are central to Native American Spirituality.
10. Explain the concept of Native American spirituality.
11. Explain the statement, "Medicine is everywhere" as it relates to Native American spirituality.
12. Why does Native American spirituality place great emphasis on the numbers four and seven?
13. Discuss the circle of life. How does it relate to the concept of relation?
14. Explain the statement, "There is no single gay identity."
15. Discuss the relationship to the West African trickster in slave culture to gay culture.
16. Discuss how mainstream culture tend to react to the discovery that an accomplished, highly regarded artist is gay?
17. What similarities does Bronski find between the African slave culture and the the gay culture?
18. How do sex and gender differ?
19. What is gender socialization?

20. How do the games of boys and girls differ and do such differences influence their communication patterns?

21. Using the examples provided by Wood and Reich, describe why men and women often have problems communicating?

22. How can men and women communicate more effectively?

23. Identify and describe the common communication thread among grandparent/grandchildren relationships that makes them so rewarding for both parties.

24. According to McKay, can we transcend the stereotypes of our aging population? If so, how, If not, why not? What is your personal belief?

25. Explain why McKay believes friendships are important to the elderly.

26. What accounts for the rise in the number of persons with disabilities?

27. What's the difference between being disabled and handicapped?

28. What have been some problems with research on disabled persons' communication?

29. Describe the different ways that one becomes a member of the disabled culture?

30. What role does language play in the redefinition of disability for disabled and temporarily able-bodied persons?

31. What suggestions do Braithwaite and Braithwaite give for communicating with people with disabilities?

32. Using information from each of the articles in Chapter 3, how are nondominant U.S. cultures such as women, African Americans, people with disabilities, gays and lesbians, and the elderly kept from obtaining equality, power, and respect by the "dominating culture"?

33. What do nondominant cultures such as women, African Americans, people with disabilities, gays and lesbians, and the elderly have in common?

34. What must nondominant cultures do in order to survive and communicate within a society that is dominated by white, male, heterosexual, and able-bodied persons?

35. How is communication affected when people from the African American and disabled communities perceive others as interacting with them using stereotypical views?

36. Taking the articles as a group, what suggestions can you give for communicating with members of nondominant U. S. cultures? Are there any suggestions that hold true for all of the cultures discussed in this chapter?

Chapter References

Dear Abby. (1993, June 24). The Seattle Times, p. 8.

de Leon, F. M., & Macdonald, S. (1992, June 28). Name Power. The Seattle Times-Seattle Post-Intelligencer, p. A1.

Jankowski, K. (1992). On Communicating with Deaf People. In L. A. Samovar and R. E. Porter (Eds.), Intercultural Communication: A Reader (5th ed.) (pp. 142-150). Belmont, CA: Wadsworth..

Part 3
Intercultural Interaction: Taking Part in Intercultural Communication

Chapter 4
Verbal Processes: Speaking Across Cultures

Chapter Synopsis

The underlying premise of this chapter is that there is an important connection between culture and language. While some may argue that the primary linguistic difference between cultures is located in grammatical structures, the contention of this chapter is that language is much more than a set of words and phrases. The articles included in this chapter address the belief that in order to understand a culture, it is important to understand not only the grammatical structure of the primary language of the culture, but the ways in which members of that culture learn and actually use language on a day-to-day basis. Understanding language as it occurs in a particular situation provides a window through which a variety of aspects of culture can be viewed. The articles in this chapter will help readers understand that knowing how different cultures use language can be just as informative as knowledge of the native language itself

Throughout this chapter students will be introduced to several variations on the theme of the interconnection between language and culture. In addition, they will have the opportunity to learn about a variety of forms of verbal communication that are found among and between cultures, After reading this chapter students should be able to articulate the perspective that members of a particular culture, as well as students exploring cultures, learn their culture through language.

Johnson examines the Language-Centered Perspective on Culture. This perspective offers us a way to holistically make sense of the many patterns of language that exist in the United States. She compares this view of culture with others in her article. Fong begins her article providing definitions of language, communication, and culture. In her article she describes the Sapir-Whorf Hypothesis. Throughout the article Fong uses examples from research on the Chinese culture to demonstrate the connection between language, communication, and culture. Zhong reviews five main eras in Chinese history. She discusses the social and political events that influenced the language of each era. The examples provided are those of Chinese native speakers as well as the author's personal experiences.

Cargile explains that culture misunderstandings can occur even when people speak the same language. He notes that language is complex and involves more than just definitions. He Reviews three major differences and how they might impact interactions between people from different cultures. Ellis and Maoz review cultural communication codes in order to establish dialogue between the Israeli-Jews and Palestinians. Arab language is reviewed as an example of a language that incorporates speech codes that help speakers work toward harmonious relationships. Finally, Roy explores Mexican values through her review of *dichos* (popular sayings). Several examples are provided to assist students with a better understanding of Mexican values.

Discussion Ideas

1. Several researchers and scholars have abandoned the idea of linguistic relativity in order to focus on analysis of discourse. Do you feel that diversity in language categories and structure lead to cultural differences in thought and perceptions of the world? In what ways might linguistic relativity affect current analysis of discourse?
2. What are the six axioms in the Language-Centered Perspective on Culture?
3. Explain the Sapir-Whorf hypothesis. How do the examples provided by Fong from her own culture contribute to your understanding of this hypothesis.
4. How do the Chinese and Americans communicate differently?
5. How do popular sayings reflect values in cultures? What popular sayings from your culture reflect values that you hold?
6. By reviewing Mexican *dichos* one can understand the Mexican culture's significant values. What are some of those values and how are they reflected in *dichos*?

Exercises

Exercise 4.1: Words Are Outside, Meanings Are Inside. This activity can be used with Fong's article exploring different perceptions on the connection between language and culture. Because people come to an interaction with different perceptions about the world, they will not understand exactly the same thing when they hear or use a word. Even among culturally similar individuals, perceptions will differ and the meanings we ascribe to the words we use will not always be shared by those who are like us. The maxim "meanings are in people" refers to the notion that words do not hold meaning, people hold meaning. Words allow us to get our meanings across to others but they do not by themselves constitute meaning, We give words meaning based on our experiences, experiences that are often culture-specific. This exercise helps demonstrate the interconnection of language, meaning, experience, and culture.

This exercise asks students to reflect on what meanings they hold of certain words and how those meanings might differ from those held by people of other cultural groups. Ask students to characterize what they think the following words mean to them by using each in a complete, "illustrative" sentence: preacher, atheist, feminist, communism, Texan, capitalism, liberal, lesbian, sexist, and bigot. Add words that you feel would be especially suited for this exercise. By "illustrative" we mean a definition that illustrates or characterizes *to students* what these labels or concepts mean. For example, for the word *teenager* someone might write: "Someone who doesn't listen to their parents, doesn't trust anyone over thirty, and believes they are invincible." After students write a sentence for each word, ask them to share their responses with a group of their classmates.

Some questions to ask students during their small group or a class discussion: How did you arrive at your own meaning of each of the words? What differences and similarities were there among the sentences? What might account for such differences and similarities? Do you think your definitions are shared by most or few people in the U.S.? Who do you think would share your definitions? Have you ever had a conversation with someone from your own culture or another culture who had a very different meaning for a word than your own definition? How might the differences we ascribe to certain words and concepts affect our interactions with people who do not share our cultural background?

Exercise 4.2: Idiomatic Expressions. This activity can be used with Roy's article on *dichos* (popular sayings) or as a way to introduce the language unit to your students. This exercise demonstrates the difficulty in explaining and translating idioms to people who do not come from the same culture. Students will learn that idioms are *very* culture-bound and that knowing a language such as English does not ensure that one will understand all the idioms of the English language. This activity can be carried out in several ways. One way is to ask students to generate their own list of idioms and explain their definitions. Divide the class into groups of four to six students. Ask them to generate as many English idioms as they can think of from the U. S. This may be difficult at first because idioms are such a natural, unconscious part of conversation so it might be wise to give a few examples to get students started. Having international students in your classroom will enhance this exercise because many of them may not be familiar with all U.S. idioms. Students will discover that many idioms are difficult to define because native speakers of any language know the idioms of their culture intuitively through years of usage. Discuss the possible origins for the idioms that students generate.

A second way to carry out this activity is to use the handout that follows entitled "Idiomatic Expressions in English" that lists English idioms from three different cultures: the United States, Great Britain, and the Bahamas. Ask students to first explain what the U. S. idioms mean. Again, international students may act as "judges" who determine whether the explanation of an idiom is adequate and whether understanding has been achieved. Then ask students to try to define the idioms in the other two lists. Which do they know, which can they accurately guess the meanings of, and which do they not understand? Give them the definitions to the British and Bahamian idioms and discuss possible reasons why these idioms were constructed the way they were.

Possible questions for discussion: Why is it difficult to explain idioms from our own culture? How do you think idioms are formed? Why do they cause a great deal of trouble for normative speakers of any language? Can you think of any idioms from the U.S. that you used to not understand but now do? Could these idioms have been regionally based? How did you come to understand each of these idioms? Did you ask for an explanation, or was the meaning clear contextually?

Exercise 4.2: Idiomatic Expressions in English

UNITED STATES

bite the dust
blow off steam
bone to pick
blow the whistle on
bored to tears
bread and butter
break the ice
brush off
beat around the bush
change one's tune
chip on one's shoulder
climb on the bandwagon

face the music
fair-weather friend
fed up
fine-tooth comb
get one's feet wet
get through one's head
feet on the ground
give up the ship
go against the grin
go to pot
in the family way
in the long run

keep your shirt on
land on ones feet
make no bones
neither here nor there
on the fence
on the whole
pay the piper
read between the lines
scratch the surface
save one's breath
miss the boat
take a back seat

GREAT BRITAIN

applaud to the echo
in bad odour
to be on (off) the beam
chop and change
as cold as charity
have a crow to pluck (pick)
die in harness
dree one's weird
hang on a person's lips
come to heel

feel like a giant refreshed
of the first water
go to one's account
not as green as he's cabbage
    looking
help a lame dog over a stile
a pretty pass
improve the occasion
have one's knife in a person
late in the field

lose the day
merry as a cricket
with might and main
grasp the nettle
put in one's oar
shilly-shally
from pillar to post
pink of perfection
to stump up
lose caste

THE BAHAMAS

bitch up
butter for fat
clap somebody up
cut up with someone
what the diggins
don't-care- -
fowled of doing something

in quest
lay on your chest/stomach
mix fool with sense
pick somebody's mouth

broad-speaking
that's chalk
cold in the arm, leg
cut your grass
dive up
draw hand
pick up gap seed

keep somebody hot
make him know
one mind tell me
pick up for somebody

get burned up
cheek somebody up
curry-favor someone
decide your mind
doggy after someone
eat off someone
grind somebody up in your
heart
land somebody off
make your break
own something to somebody
pitch a stink

Exercise 4.2: Idiomatic Expressions in English

Key

GREAT BRITAIN (Collins, 1958)
Note: some of these may no longer be used in everyday conversation.

applaud to the echo: to acclaim and clap loudly, so that one rouses echoes.

in bad odour: in disfavour, in disrepute.

to be on/off the beam: to be on or off the point, to be relevant or irrelevant.

chop and change: to be constantly changing, generally used derogatorily.

come to keel: to show humble and complete obedience.

feel like a giant refreshed: to feel physically or morally strong after something has happened.

as cold as charity: lacking in signs of warm emotion.

have a crow to pluck (pick): to have a complaint or criticism to make.

die in harness: to die while still actively engaged in the course of one's regular work.

dree one's weird: to endure with philosophic resignation what happens to one ("weird" is used here in place of fate).

hang on a person's lips: to listen closely to; similar to *hang on a person's every word*

of the first water: of the most excellent kind.

go to one's account: to die.

not as green as he's cabbage-looking: not so simple as one might think: not such a fool as he looks.

help a lame dog over a stile: help a person deal with a difficulty with which he/she is incapable of coping.

a pretty pass: a serious state of affairs.

improve the occasion: to seize every advantage one can out of the circumstance.

have one's knife in a person: to be constantly finding occasions for complaining about or blaming a person.

late in the field: late on the scene.

lose caste: to forfeit one social position by doing something that is regarded as socially discreditable.

lose the day: to be defeated.

merry as a cricke:. extremely cheerful.

with might and main: with all one's power.

grasp the nettle: to tackle a difficulty or danger boldly.

put in one's oar:. to intervene in action or discussion.

shilly-shally: to vacillate, waver, be undecided, hesitate.

from pillar to post: to move from one place or resource to another.

pink of perfection: the highest degree of what is perfect of its kind.

to stump up: to pay money.

Exercise 4.2: Idiomatic Expressions in English

Key

BAHAMAS (Holm, 1982)

bitch up: to ruin, spoil; to frustrate.

broad-speaking: plain-speaking, outspoken.

get burned up: to become exhausted through physical exertion.

butter-for-fat: like for like; similar to *tit-for tat.*

that's chalk: that's inevitable- a foregone conclusion- slang for *that's great.*

cheek somebody up: to be impertinent to somebody.

clap somebody up: to applaud somebody; similar to *applaud to the echo.*

cold in the arm, leg: an inflammation of the arm or leg.

curry-favor someone: give somebody an unfair advantage because of personal connections; curry somebody's favor.

cut-up with someone: to flirt.

cut your grass: to usurp someone else's prerogative or exclusive right or privilege.

decide your mind: to make a decision.

what the diggins: an exclamation of surprise.

dive up: to dive into the water and bring something up.

doggy **after someone:** to follow someone about constantly.

don't-care-'f-I: not caring, especially about social norms.

draw hand: to make a leading or beckoning gesture.

eat off someone: to eat at someone else's expense.

fowled of **doing something:** engaged in doing something.

pick up gap seed: to gather information for gossip.

grind somebody up in your heart. to bear a grudge against somebody.

in quest:. to admit defeat in playing cards or marbles.

keep somebody hot: to be at a person' s heals, getting in his/her way.

land somebody **off**. to drop someone off from a car or boat.

lay on your chest/stomach: to cause indigestion or nightmares (of food eaten late at night).

make him know: to scold or punish.

make your break: to seize an opportunity to do what one has been wanting to do.

mix fool with **sense:** to attempt to deceive someone by interspersing lies with the truth.

one mind tell me: I had a vague contradictory feeling (that something would happen, etc.).

own something to somebody: to confess something to somebody.

pick somebody's mouth: to get information by engaging in seemingly casual conversation.

pick up for somebody: to take somebody's side of the argument.

pitch a stink: to object vehemently, cause a commotion.

Exercise 4.3: Popular Sayings . This activity is designed to be used in conjunction with the Roy article on Mexican *dichos* (popular sayings). *Dichos* are one way that a culture teaches its members appropriate conduct, including effective ways of communication. Consider this cultural proverb well known to people in the United States: 'You scratch my back, I'll scratch yours." This saying alludes to a rule of negotiation based on compromise and give and take. The Zairean proverb, "A little subtleness is better than a lot of force" suggests to members of this African culture that one should not be too pushy and overbearing when communicating. Proverbs are one way that our culture passes on wisdom. Roy discusses *dichos* that are specific to the Mexican culture. Have your students share some specific popular sayings that their families have taught them. For example, many Jewish children hear the proverb that "With money in your pocket, you are wise and you are handsome and you sing well too." Have students identify how these familial proverbs have impacted their lives. Be aware of any contrasting proverbs among the students. For example, "Honesty is the best policy" versus "Little white lies never hurt anyone." Contrasting proverbs can lead to a lively discussion when their implications are analyzed by the class.

Exercise 4.4: Cultural Attitudes Toward Speakers--How Do Others Perceive Us? This exercise is meant to accompany Cargile's article on discriminating attitudes toward speech. It asks students to imagine how others might perceive them culturally and individually based on: their: accent, speech style, and rate of speech. The objective of this exercise is to make students aware of how others might perceive them when they speak in an intercultural setting and how closely these perceptions match students' own perceptions of their cultural and personal characteristics. It is also designed to have them evaluate their own practices of judging and forming attitudes towards others based on these same speech characteristics. Have students answer the following questions individually. Impress upon them that they are to imagine, as much as possible, how *others* would perceive them, not how they perceive themselves. It might be helpful for students if they would imagine an intercultural encounter with a differently-accented person or group of people that they have had previously.

1.   List five *cultural* characteristics that you think differently-accented others would use to describe you after hearing you speak.
2.   List five *individual* characteristics that they would use to describe you in this same situation.

Afterwards, the class may be separated into small discussion groups, and/or a class discussion may follow. Have students share some of their answers. Possible questions for discussion: What characteristics of your speech would lead people to make these assumptions about you? How would their assumptions be right or wrong? In your imagination, were these differently-accented folks standard or nonstandard speakers? Would they have labeled you a standard or a nonstandard speaker? What cultural markers best explain the difference between your speech and the speech of those others you imagined? In other words, were the differences due to different nationalities, races, socioeconomic levels, etc.? How does their particular brand of "otherness" relate to you in terms of a social structure invested with power? In other words, who is considered more powerful in the interaction? Who is in the privileged position? Do you think that their impression of you is accurate? How similar are their cultural and individual predictions? How different are they? Where are the contradictions? In what situations do you think it would be useful to make cultural predictions or assumptions based on a person's speech? Individual predictions and assumptions? When are both most useful? When are both most dangerous or destructive? Is it possible for people to suspend this practice of judgment once they have identified it for themselves? If so, would that be desirable or not? Why?

Exercise 4.5: Interruption or Conversational Overlap? Deborah Tannen (1986), a noted researcher in language and communication, explains that there are no universal rules for politeness during conversations. She explains that some people find it impolite to talk at the same time as someone else. For other people, however, an overlap is not perceived as an interruption but as a way for showing enthusiasm and understanding. Whether or not we feel simultaneous talk is merely an overlap or an actual interruption during conversations is often determined by the conversational norms established in the cultural communities in which we are members. This exercise asks students to reflect on their perceptions of conversational norms and those of other cultures by listening to tape-recorded interactions.

Overlaps are generally understood as moments when a new speaker attempts to take the floor during a conversation when a another speaker is finishing or is perceived as being close to completing his or her turn. Overlaps can also be times when a listener becomes more actively involved in a conversation by making comments during a speaker's turn at talk. It is very common for words to overlap during these conversational moments. An interruption may be perceived as something more abrasive and often used for purposes of cutting the person off and gaining the floor. An interruption may also, however, be perceived favorably, not at all intrusive, and even as expected communicative behavior. How do students perceive and use overlaps and interruptions during their own conversations? Have they noticed differences in the way certain cultural groups use overlaps and interruptions in their talk?

Gather two tape-recorded conversations, one that distinctly displays interruptions and the other that includes overlaps but no interruptions. If possible, gather these samples from two different cultural communities or from conversations that include members from two or more cultural groups. Although transcriptions of portions of the conversation would be helpful for students as they listen, they are not necessary. Have students listen to the conversations. Facilitate a discussion with the class using some of the following questions: Where are the overlaps? the interruptions? What makes these overlaps and interruptions? How would you interpret these overlaps and interruptions? What are the "overlapper" and the "interrupter" attempting to do? Using the responses of the persons being overlapped and interrupted as information, how do you think they are interpreting these behaviors? How might the culture of the interactants influence their perceptions of these overlaps and interruptions? How is your culture influencing your perceptions of this conversation? How are overlaps and interruptions interpreted in your culture(s)? Does it depend on who you are talking with? Does formality, role, and familiarity influence the extent to which overlaps and interruptions are used and how they are interpreted? How can people from different cultures who have different conversational norms communicate effectively?

Exercise 4.6: Case Studies on Language. The following activity is designed to illustrate for students how the same word or phrase can have very different meanings for individuals from different cultures. Students will understand that the simplest and taken-for-granted words and phrases in one culture can pose a problem in an intercultural interaction if different meanings are ascribed to the same verbal message. This activity can be done in groups or individually. Ask students to read the following case studies. Both case studies deal with a situation depicting a Kenyan and an individual from the U.S. interacting. Have them answer the questions that follow each case study.

Case Study #1

Joanna was a Peace Corps volunteer in Kenya who had just recently arrived at her site. She was anxious to meet many of the people of the community quickly and spent her first days riding her motorcycle through the hills near her house. While riding she stopped to talk with a Kenyan man named Kimani. They had a pleasant conversation and Kimani asked if they could talk again sometime because he was anxious to hear more about the United States. Joanna was eager to establish some friendships while in Kenya and told Kimani that she was glad to have found a friend. Kimani stopped by Joanna's house the next day and stayed for several hours. He visited Joanna regularly and brought her small gifts. Joanna realized quickly that Kimani wished to develop more than a friendship with her. She decided to discuss their relationship with him.

"Kimani, I think we need to talk about our friendship."
"Yes."
"I think you might want something more than I do, you know, something
 more serious."
"You said you wanted us to be friends, right? That's what I want too."
"I guess I don't quite understand Kenyan customs yet. Do you bring gifts to your friends every time you visit them?"
"If I want to have a girlfriend, someone special, I do."
"But I thought you just wanted us to be friends."
"That's right, I do. I want us to be friends. That's why I am visiting you and bringing you gifts."

(1)   What word is the cause of Joanna and Kimani's confusion?
(2)   Explain why they are miscommunicating.
(3)   How would you continue this dialogue to solve this intercultural dilemma?

Case Study #2

Michael had just arrived at his school in Kenya. He was assigned to teach science at a rural high school outside of Kisumu. Charles, one of his students, visited him one Friday afternoon after school and they had a nice chat while drinking tea. As Charles was leaving, Michael waved to him and said, "See you later!" The following Monday, Charles approached Michael appearing confused.

"Mwalimu, I was waiting for you Friday evening but you never came."
"Was I supposed to meet you somewhere, Charles?"
"Well, I thought you were going to visit me at my home."
"Really? I don't remember telling you that Friday afternoon."
"You said that you would see me later so I thought that you would come visit me later that evening."
"Charles, I don't remember telling you that. Are you sure I said that?"

(1)   What phrase is the cause of Charles and Michael's confusion?
(2)   Explain why they are miscommunicating?
(3)   How would you continue this dialogue to solve this intercultural dilemma?

The first case study dealt with the word "friend" and the different meanings of "friend" being used by Joanna and Kimani. The word "friend" can have an additional meaning for Kenyans besides denoting an individual with whom one has a platonic relationship (the typical U.S. definition.) For many Kenyans, to say someone of the opposite sex is your friend can also mean that you are having a romantic or intimate relationship with this person. The second case study focused on the use of the common U.S. leave-taking phrase, "See you later!" Charles was probably not familiar with this idiomatic expression and took the phrase literally. Michael did not even remember having used this phrase because he said it almost unconsciously and was using it strictly to mean "good-bye" or "until we meet again."

Questions for discussion: Why do people attribute different meanings to the same word or phrase? Can any one word or phrase have one meaning? Or are there a number of definitions for every word and phrase? What role does experience and culture have in ascribing meaning to words and phrases? How do these case studies support the idea that language and experience are inextricably linked? What often happens when idioms are taken literally? Can you think of greetings, farewell phrases, and other small talk "niceties" that are used in your culture? Have you ever stopped to think what they might mean to someone who does not come from your culture? Have you ever heard an idiom that you didn't understand? Have you ever used a phrase or idiom that another person interpreted differently than you had intended?

Test Items for Chapter 4

Multiple Choice

1.   Which of the following statements is true about culture?
    a.   cultures comprise symbolic systems that create webs of meaning.
    b.   cultures endure over long periods
    c.   cultures are learned by humans through both explicit instruction and tacit acquisition
    d.   all of the above *

2.   Most U.S. citizens expressed outrage with the punishment of Michael Fay in 1994 for spray painting in Singapore because
    a.   Americans thought the punishment did not match the crime *
    b.   Americans thought the punishment was not long enough
    c.   Americans thought the punishment was too severe
    d.   Americans thought the punishment should have been harsher

3.   Qualitative research methods examine the interrelationship of language and culture through
    a.   ethnography.
    b.   pragmatics.
    c.   discourse analysis.
    d.   all of the above. *

4.   The unfortunate incident of breaking a glass object during Chinese New Year is transformed to a fortunate incident when
    a.   the object is replaced.
    b.   the person breaking the object says a prayer.
    c.   the person orally uses a positive expression to describe the unfortunate act. *
    d.   by redescribing the incident as a purposeful gesture.

5.   Diversity in language categories and structure lead to cultural differences in thought is known as
    a.   linguistic relativity *
    b.   linguistic subjectivity
    c.   linguistic differences
    d.   none of the above

6. Which of the following approaches focuses on the underlying factors that influence language choices in multilingual communication contexts?
    a.   the developmental approach
    b.   the interactional approach
    c.   the social psychological approach *
    d.   none of the above

7. Brown (1958) disagreed with the Sapir-Whorf hypothesis because
    a.   he believed people categorized their world by attaching labels to what is out there *
    b.   he believed there was no basis for the hypothesis
    c.   he believed there was not a reliable way to measure their hypothesis
    d.   none of the above

8. Chinese immigrant participants are described as being in which state when they are unfamiliar with European Americans' generosity?
    a.   intercultural shock state *
    b.   intercultural resistance state
    c.   intercultural accommodation state
    d.   bi-cultural competence state

9. Which of the following eras is recognized as the beginning of contemporary Chinese history?
    a.   The New Culture Era *
    b.   The New China Era
    c.   The Cultural Revolution Era
    d.   The Economic Reform Era

10. The first decade or so after the founding of the People's Republic of China was regarded as
    a.   The New Culture Era
    b.   The New China Era *
    c.   The Cultural Revolution Era
    d.   The Economic Reform Era

11. During which era was the college entrance exam reestablished in China allowing young people to take the exam regardless of class status or family background?
    a.   the New Culture era
    b.   the New China era
    c.   the Cultural Revolution era
    d.   the Economic Reform era *

12. In the 1990's a Chinese delegation followed the secretary around for directions during their visit to a university department in the United States because
    a. they did not want to disturb the department chairperson
    b. they assumed the secretary was in charge of the department *
    c. they thought the secretary was the person that had the most time available
    d. none of the above

13. The word "lao" is used after someone's last name in China when
    a. you are extremely well established and have earned high respect *
    b. for people over fifty
    c. for young people around 20 and 30
    d. for middle aged people around 40 to 50

14. In Seggie's 1983 study of listener responses to standard and nonstandard voices, standard-accented speakers were more often seen as guilty of _____, whereas nonstandard-accented speakers were more often seen as guilty of

    _____.
    a. embezzlement, physical assault *
    b. domestic abuse, street violence
    c. embezzlement, robbery
    d. tax evasion, physical assault

15. According to Cargile, our attitudes toward language and their influence on intercultural communication can be traced to which of the following characteristics?
    a. accents
    b. speech styles
    c. speech rates
    d. all of the above *

16. Which of the following is not considered a communication feature of musayra?
    a. repetition
    b. indirectness
    c. elaboration
    d. clarification *

17. Which of the following statements is not true?
    a. speech codes are culturally distinctive
    b. speech codes result from a psychology and sociology unique to the culture
    c. speech codes are located in the language and communication of native speakers
    d. speech codes cannot be used to understand, predict, and control communication *

18. The contact hypothesis is optimal when
    a. two groups are of unequal status
    b. successful contact should involve personal and sustained communication between individuals from the two groups *
    c. two groups do not have to depend on one another
    d. none of the above

19. Dichos, popular sayings, have an impact on human behavior because
    a. they reflect many of the basic values of contemporary Mexican society.
    b. they capture what a culture deems important.
    c. they are handed down from one generation to the next.
    d. all of the above *

20. "No por mucho madrugar amancee mas temprano" , (no matter how early the sun rises, the sun will not come up any sooner) can be interpreted to mean that

    a. one must simply accept what one cannot change *
    b. if you don't rise early, you will miss out on a lot
    c. if you rise early, you will not miss out on anything
    d. one must simply accept what life brings

21. According to Roy's article about Mexican *dichos* which of the following is not a significant value in the Mexican culture?
    a. cheerful acceptance of one's lot
    b. the need to exercise caution when placing trust
    c. the unimportance of appearances *
    d. the sanctity of privacy

True/False

T   1.   Cultural Artifacts express their particular cultural frameworks and sometimes rebel against them.
T   2.   All communication, whether verbal or nonverbal, occurs within cultural frameworks.
T   3.   Cultures are dynamic rather than static.
T   4.   According to the Sapir-Whorf hypothesis, language influences and shapes how people perceive their world and their culture.
F   5.   In general, the Sapir-Whorf hypothesis has come to be regarded as confirmable and correct.
F   6.   Chinese immigrants value immodesty and have little problem accepting direct compliments from Americans.

T	7.	Chinese employ language to reverse bad luck.
F	8.	Developmental theorists are interested in identifying appropriate communication styles and norms in various cultures.
F	9.	When Chinese Immigrant Participants were found to be in the Intercultural shock state they became very verbal participants.
T	10.	No other known language has existed and retained its structure over such a long history than Chinese.
F	11.	In the 1990's Chinese did not accept many Western words in their original forms into their vocabulary.
T	12.	Research has shown that listeners make ready and regular judgments regarding the personal and social characteristics of speakers based simply on the way they sound.
T	13.	In universities across America, students often respond unfavorably to foreign-born teaching assistants and professors.
T	14.	*Musraya* means "to accommodate" or "go along with".
F	15.	An Arab speaker who is engaging in the code of *musraya* is being impolite, direct, uncourteous and confrontive.
T	16.	*Dugri* is the opposite of *musayra.*
T	17.	*Dugri* and *musayra* are excellent examples of speech codes.
T	18.	Speech codes can be used to understand, predict, and control communication.
T	19.	Israeli-Jews qualify their arguments, backtrack, and provide context.
F	20.	The Israelis engage in something known as "tag-team" arguments.
T	21.	Dichos are a form of transmitting folk wisdom.
F	22.	Through *dichos* we are reminded that our experiences are unique.

Essay Questions

1. Differentiate between the Enlightenment and Romantic views as ways of approaching culture.
2. Explain cultural abstractions and provide examples to substantiate your response.
3. Explain the role jewelry plays as a cultural artifact and provide examples of jewelry as worn in a variety of cultures.
4. Discuss the link between language and culture. Provide examples to support your response.
5. Explain the following formula "If … then… because… meaning" when referring to the Chinese custom of reversing negative comments.
6. Explain how the Chinese deal with compliment interactions.
7. How do Chinese and Americans express themselves differently? Provide examples for support.
8. Explain how the Chinese language reflects the structure of the society.
9. What can be done about discriminating attitudes toward speech? In your response, provide specific ways the text suggests that responsible intercultural communicators do about these attitudes?
10. Under what conditions is the contact hypothesis optimal?

11. Explain the concept of "dialogue" when used when groups are in conflict.

12. Explain how your use of language and your tendencies to interpret and understand this language in a certain way depends on your cultural membership. Provide examples to substantiate your response.

13. Explain the concept of two cultural communication codes termed *dugri* and *musayra* which are known to characterize the Israeli-Jews and Arabs.

14. Identify and explain the four communication features of *musraya*..

15. Discuss the well-documented code, *dugri,* used by the Israeli-Jews.

16. Explain *dugri* and *musraya* within the context of the five principles of speech codes.

17. Explain the popular Mexican sayings "*Aqua que no has beber, dejala corer* (Water that you do not have to drink, leave it to flow.) and *En boca cerrada no entran moscas*. (Flies do not enter a closed mouth.)

18. Explain the importance of family in the Mexican culture. Provide an example of one *dicho* that speaks to the importance of family.

Cultural Dialogs

Chapter References

Collins, V. H. (1958). <u>A second book of English idioms</u>. London: Longmans, Green and Co.

Holm, J. A. (1982). Dictionary of Bahamian English. New York: Lexik House Publishers.

Tannen, D. (1986). <u>That's not what I meant! How conversational style makes or breaks relationships</u>. New York: Ballantine.

Chapter 5
Nonverbal Interaction: Action, Sound, and Silence

Chapter Synopsis

The major premise of this chapter is that successful intercultural communication requires more than an understanding of verbal interaction. Nonverbal behavior also provides important insight into cultural patterns of communication. In this chapter students will be introduced to the role and impact of movement, personal space, touch, time, gender, paralanguage and silence in a variety of cultural contexts. As the editors note, nonverbal communication often serves as the frame for interpreting verbal communication, so learning about some of the patterns of communicating without words offers students of intercultural communication a broader understanding of communication among and between cultures.

The assumption that nonverbal behaviors are for the most part unconscious behaviors undergirds this chapter. It is important for students to note that any portrayal of the nonverbal behaviors described as typical from one culture to the next are not characterizations of behaviors that are formally "taught" within each culture. Students who wish to communicate more effectively interculturally should not expect to "learn" appropriate nonverbal behaviors simply by reading about them in the text. Rather, what this text offers is a way of viewing behaviors that students might otherwise misinterpret for noncommunicative events.

Andersen's article provides a thorough overview of nonverbal communication and its relationship to culture. He explains that nonverbal codes shift from culture to culture. McDaniel uses the Japanese as a cultural model to illustrate how nonverbal communication practices function as a reflection, or representation of societal cultural themes. Students will learn how cultural influences can subtlety shape a society's nonverbal communication behavior. Hall provides an interesting description of time as a nonverbal feature of communication. Again, students may find themselves wondering about the ways in which time is a communicative variable among cultures. Hall's distinction between monochromic and polychronic time introduces students to some of the interaction forms that may emerge as a result of cultural differences regarding time. Finally, Borisoff and Merrill synthesize communication scholarship on gender and nonverbal communication. Their article exposes the role of power in nonverbal interactions between women and men in the U.S. Each section of the article ends with a call for students to challenge their own complicity with normalizing cultural scripts for gendered, nonverbal communication.

Discussion Ideas

1.   According to Andersen, "culture is primarily a nonverbal phenomenon." To what extent do you agree or disagree with his conclusion?

      a.   If we are to accept his claim that culture is not learned through explicit verbal instruction, what value is there in training people to be more interculturally aware?

b.   Encourage students to think about their own experiences with other cultures. If they say that they have never had any experience with a culture other than their own, suggest that they think about organizations, classrooms, and families as cultures. How have they learned how to behave appropriately in new cultures? Via explicit verbal instruction or by watching and learning through repeated observation of what people do?

2.   What does it mean to say that one culture is more masculine than another? What is the relationship between the communication that occurs in cultures labeled as masculine and the role of women within the culture? The role of men?

3.   Many people assume that we can learn to read a person's nonverbal communication like a book. There are even popular press books published on the subject. Andersen argues that we cannot read members of our own cultures let alone members of another culture. To what extent do you agree or disagree with his conclusion?

4.   How might the homogeneity of the Japanese affect consistent themes in society? Compare the Japanese situation to that in the U.S.?

5.   What problems would you anticipate between dating partners, one of whom comes from a high-context culture and the other from a low-context culture?

6.   Hall differentiates between monochromic and polychronic time, indicating that different cultures operate with different perspectives of time. Do you feel that these orientations to time are limited to cultural distinctions or do individuals operate on different times as well? What are some of the potential ramifications for business and personal interactions when parties to the communicative event have different perceptions of time?

7.   How are nonverbal factors of communication between and among cultures related to the verbal components of language discussed in the previous chapter?

8.   Given the complexity of language, what advice would you have for someone who hopes to not only understand, but take part in the day-to-day life of another culture?

9.   Were you genuinely surprised by any of the claims made in Borisoff and Merrill's article on gender and nonverbal communication? Did they describe communication scenarios that you have experienced? Did their descriptions cause you to reevaluate this experience? As a culture, which nonverbal communication behaviors discussed by the authors must we challenge first? Why are these most significant to you? How could we challenge and begin to change these dynamics? Give concrete examples. As an individual, is there something in particular that you want to change about your own nonverbal communication behaviors? Why? How will you accomplish this?

10.   Borisoff and Merrill are careful to point out that both gender roles and nonverbal communication styles are culturally specific; however, their article is primarily concerned

with the cultural context of America. Have you lived in or visited other cultures where nonverbal behaviors and gender roles differ significantly from those in the U.S.? Give concrete examples. Based one your knowledge of the relationship between nonverbal behaviors and power relations, who is in the relative position of power in the scenario you have described? Who is in the less powerful position? Does this tell you something about that cultures larger power structure or not? Please explain your answer.

Exercises

Exercise 5 1: Nonverbal Greeting/Leave-Taking Behaviors. This activity is designed to incorporate all the articles in chapter 5 by heightening the students' awareness of how they take part in greeting and leave-taking behaviors and how these behaviors might be vastly different from other cultures of the world. This exercise will also make students aware of their own level of comfort in touching and being touched as well as their preferred space distance. Begin by dividing the class into two subgroups, X and Y, which represent groups of business professionals from two different cultures. Distinguish the two groups with something obvious such as colorful armbands, nametags, or ribbons. Ask Team Y to leave the room. You may give the teams written or verbal instructions.

Instruct Team X members that when Team Y comes back into the room they are to meet and greet their friends and business associates who are Team Y members. Inform Team X members that they come from a culture where close contact and warm embraces are the traditional style of saying "hello." Point out that when they shake hands on encountering Team Y members they must prolong the handshake for a least thirty seconds. Then they should make small talk for a few minutes (ask about family members, school, sports etc. but do not engage in discussions of business, instead, redirect the conversation to other non-business topics), standing a little closer than is normally comfortable for them. A bell should ring after a few minutes and then Team X should say good-bye by giving their partner a warm embrace.

Instruct Team Y members that when they reenter the room they are to meet and greet members of Team X as friends and business associates in the traditional fashion of U.S. organizational culture by shaking hands. Team Y's objective is to begin a business transaction with Team X. They should say good-bye when the bell rings by shaking hands. The entire interaction should last for no more than three to four minutes.

Facilitate a debriefing session by asking for student comments about how they felt during the exercise. Discuss the awkwardness evident when different nonverbal rules were being used during the interaction. If you have a culturally diverse classroom, you will obviously get very different responses. These responses will undoubtedly enrich the discussion by lending first-hand insight into the touch and proxemic behavior of various cultural groups. Discuss with students the extent to which members of U.S. cultures engage in public touch behavior, when, and with whom. Also, talk with students about other cultures around the globe that engage in same-sex touching in public. For example, in Kenya and Nigeria men walk hand-in-hand frequently yet mixed-sex handholding is rarely seen. In some African countries, handshakes are often extended, not the quick, firm grasps as is often the case in the U. S. Ask team Y if they felt frustrated at team X's refusal to talk about business. While U.S. business people are often in a "hurry" to get down to business, other cultures prefer to establish friendships before conducting business. This represents a different time orientation than is typical in the U.S.

Possible questions for further discussion: What happens when someone touches more than we are used to? How do we respond? Why? When do you feel comfortable hugging someone and whom do you feel comfortable hugging? Is such a greeting or goodbye appropriate for business associates? How does the amount of space between interactants impact a conversation? How much space do you like to have? What does standing closer to someone during a conversation indicate to you? How much of our nonverbal or affectionate behavior is culturally determined and how much is individually determined? How do you feel when you see two men and/or two women hugging? What happens when someone we are interacting with is on a different time orientation than our own? How do we respond? Why? What do these feelings tell us about the attitudes and behavior rules of our respective cultures? -About our individual attitudes?

Exercise 5.2: Seeing and Perceiving. This activity can be used in conjunction with Andersen's article on the cues of culture. It illustrates one cue of culture -- gaze -- and its impact on interaction and the meaning we ascribe to direct or indirect eye contact. Students will understand how they have come to interpret eye contact in culturally specific ways and how misunderstandings can arise when we misinterpret a person's intentions or level of interest based on the amount of eye contact they use. Divide students into groups of four. The groups are to engage in a directed discussion that will hopefully lead to a decision being made. Each group will receive four slips of paper with each slip having one of the following messages:

1.   You are an African-American and one of several managers in a large, multinational firm. You have asked a group of other managers to come together to generate ideas for the company's upcoming Employee Appreciation Day. You would like the group to come to a decision as to where the festivities will take place and what types of food and entertainment will be provided. Your job is to engage all group members in a discussion of the available alternatives. You and the other three managers all hold the same level of position. You engage in a lot of direct eye contact while talking, but much less eye contact when listening to a person. (*Do not attempt to use accented speech or reveal the country or culture that you are from.)

2.   You are from Japan and one of several managers in a large, multinational firm. You have been asked to join a group of managers to discuss plans for the upcoming Employee Appreciation Day. You hold the same level of position as the other three group members. You engage in a lot of indirect eye contact when speaking and listening to people. (*Do not attempt to use accented speech or reveal the country or culture that you are from.)

3.   You are a Caucasian from the United States and one of several managers in a large, multinational firm. You have been asked to join a group of managers to discuss plans for the upcoming Employee Appreciation Day. You engage in a lot of direct eye contact when listening to people but a moderate amount when

speaking to people. (*Do not attempt to use accented speech or reveal the country or culture that you are from.)

4.   You are from Saudi Arabia and one of several managers in a large, multinational firm. You have been asked to join a group of managers to discuss plans for the upcoming Employee Appreciation Day. You hold the same level of position as the other three group members. You engage in a lot of direct eye contact while speaking and your gaze is long, intense, and unbroken, (*Do not attempt to use accented speech or reveal the country or culture that you are from.)

Each group member receives one of the above four roles. Give the students time to read their roles and understand what their instructions are. The member who has called the meeting should begin the discussion and give the group a short synopsis of why they have been called together. Allow the role-play to continue for approximately fifteen to twenty minutes.

Engage the class in a discussion of what happened during the exercise. Was it difficult to role play the nonverbal behavior of a culture other than your own? What nonverbal behavioral differences did you notice among the group members? With whose nonverbal behavior did you feel comfortable? Why? With whose did you not? Why? Could you guess the culture of each individual? Did your perceptions of their nonverbal behavior match their intentions while behaving? What discrepancies were there between the sender's nonverbal behavior and the receiver's perception of the behavior? What communication problems occurred as a result of the different types of eye contact used? Can you think of times when you have felt uncomfortable with another person's nonverbal behavior (eye contact, touch, proximity, etc.)? What meanings did you ascribe to their behavior and did this meaning match their intentions? How can we become more comfortable with the nonverbal behavior of other cultures and co-cultures?

Exercise 5.3: When Another Is Silent. This activity deals with silence as a nonverbal behavior and is designed to be used with McDaniel's article on Japanese nonverbal communication as a reflection of Japanese culture. Most people have experienced a conversation where one person did most of the talking while the other took the "patient listener" role. Such experiences can lead to feelings of frustration and, sadly, sometimes to the end of developing relationships. On the other hand, it is also common to feel responsible for carrying the conversation with little assistance from a more silent friend or acquaintance. While both people in a conversation may have the responsibility of "monitoring" the extent to which they are sharing information and listening to the other share, striking a comfortable balance between the two is not always implicitly agreed upon by all individuals. The extent to which we speak and use silence in a conversation is often culturally determined.

What counts as a balance between listening and talking may be culturally determined. As has been mentioned in several articles in the *Reader,* we learn as we grow up the cultural norms of interaction. Conversational competence in one culture may include asking many questions while in another, such communicative behavior would be deemed intrusive. This case study focuses on how different cultures perceive conversation competence during the first stages of a potential romantic relationship. Read the case and answer the questions that follow. As you read, consider your own experiences on first dates…what happened? How did you interpret the other person's communications

Jonathan and Noriko were out on their first date together. They had met in one of their classes and talked with each other several times at school. On the way over to the movie theater Jonathan noticed that Noriko was rather quiet, more quiet than when he had talked with her at school. After the movie, Jonathan suggested that they have coffee at a local cafe. Noriko still did not say very much as they sipped their coffee and Jonathan found himself filling in the silences with comments about school and questions about her family and growing up in Japan. He also talked a lot about his family since he was very close with them. Even though she answered his questions with short responses and MM seem very willing to say much about her family, Noriko appeared to be in good spirits and when asked, said she was having a good time.

Jonathan dropped Noriko off at her apartment at about 11:00. They said goodnight at her door and as Jonathan got in his car, he was convinced Noriko had had a terrible time. He was worried that she hadn't said very much throughout the evening and wondered if he had offended her in some way. He talked with Noriko just before their class a few times the following week but they didn't make any plans to go out again. About a month later, after the school year had ended, Jonathan found out from a mutual friend that Noriko was disappointed that they never went out again. She said that she had really enjoyed his company and was hoping they could see each other again.

Questions for discussion: From the information above, describe the communication styles of Noriko and Jonathan. Why had Jonathan and Noriko perceived the success of their first date so differently? How might their relationship have developed differently? What could each have done to continue its development? What does quiet or silence communicate to you on a first date? Where did you get this interpretation(s)? Consider some alternative interpretations of silence. How does context and familiarity influence how we interpret their quietness or silence? Describe a time when a person you had just begun dating or had just met wasn't saying very much. How did you interpret this person's silence? Did you find out what this silence meant to this person?

Exercise 5.4: Time and Culture. The following case study is designed to be used with Hall's article on time and demonstrates the difficulties people can encounter when learning and adapting to how individuals from other cultures perceive and orient to time. How time is viewed in some cultures is not a fixed orientation but can fluctuate depending on the context and the individual.

When people conceptualize time differently, their relationships may be affected. Ask students to read the story below and answer the questions that follow. The narrator is a teacher from the United States teaching in the East African country of Uganda.

I had arranged to meet Paul at 2:00 on Saturday in front of the post office. I had been invited by his mother for tea and he was meeting me to take me to their home in the hills surrounding the small town I called home for two years. Paul was an older student who started Form One (freshman) when he was 26. Being the oldest in the family, he had been needed at home and could not attend school until he was a young man. I was looking forward to meeting his family.

I arrived at the post office at 1:00. Because it was Saturday, there were not many people in town. The busiest days were Mondays and Thursdays-market days--and the weekends tended to bring fewer people into town during the day. As I waited for Paul, I watched the people come and go as they checked their mailboxes. 2:15 came and still no Paul. I was beginning to wonder whether I had heard 2:00 or 3:00 when Paul and I spoke the day before. I was sure it was 2:00. Well, 2:30 came and I was beginning to get frustrated; then 2:45 came, and now I was angry. Why did he say 2:00 and then not show up?

As my watch clicked to exactly 2:56, I saw Paul turn the corner of one of the several butchers in town. He approached the post office, smiled, and greeted me

"It's a long walk to my home. I hope you're ready for a journey."

I said yes, half-waiting for an apology from him for being late. It never came.

"Paul, did you say you would meet me at 2:00 or 3:00?"

"I said 2:00. I hope you were not waiting long. Are you ready to go?"

Still no apology or explanation. After a very long walk we reached his home. The afternoon was wonderful and I thoroughly enjoyed meeting Paul's family. When I returned to school the following Monday, I asked one of the Kenyan teachers what she would have thought about Paul arriving almost an hour late.

"Oh, but he was not late. You said he came at 2:56. That's still 2:00."

"It's a lot closer to 3:00 than 2:00," I responded.

"Ah, perhaps in 'American time' but remember here we are on 'African time.'"

Some questions for discussion in either small groups or as a class: How had the U.S. teacher understood "African time"? How would you describe African time? American time? Do you think the U.S. teacher should have been upset with Paul? Would you have left town? Would you have said something to Paul about arriving at 2:56? What might you have said? Can you identify and describe an event during a relationship that you have had, intercultural or intracultural, that was affected by differing conceptualizations of time? How did you respond to this difference and why did you respond this way? How might you respond now under similar circumstances? Any changes?

Exercise 5.5: Culture and Conversation. To some people, conversation can be understood as an art form. Others may see it as purely functional, merely words that accomplish a set goal. How we approach conversation with other people can depend a great deal on how we have been acculturated to use and orient ourselves towards social discourse. Conversation and interpersonal relations are synonymous: when we converse we are relating interpersonally -- person to person. And as we know, conversation includes more than spoken words. The use of silence and space, and the conceptualization of time, also make up the "stuff" of conversation.

This activity illustrates how the use of space, silence, and time during conversation can greatly affect intercultural relations and perceptions of other cultures. Ask students to read each of the conversational descriptions given below and envision a scenario where members from both cultures are engaging in conversation. This exercise can also be done by using the descriptions below in a dialogue and having two or more students role play an interaction in front of the class.

Culture A

Talking is synonymous with productivity in this culture. When one talks with another, something useful and functional is taking place. If there is talk, then something is being accomplished. Periods of silence are not looked upon favorably, are perceived as awkward moments, and generally a waste of time because silence makes use time in an unproductive way.

If people are not talking, questions are asked or the subject is changed in an attempt to continue the flow of words. Curt, hurried language is the norm. Conversation in this culture is also marked by considerable distance (approximately three feet) between two individuals. It is considered extremely rude to "get in people's faces."

Culture B

This culture views talk as something quite special, not to be overused for fear it may be tread upon or misused. Talk is not how a person displays wisdom or shows the "true" self. "The one who talks knows little and reveals only falsehoods" is a common saying. Silence is what wise people engage in because knowledge lies within the individual, not on the outside. People respect intuition and introspection.

When members of this culture do talk, they are brief but clear, simple but eloquent. Words are unique objects that must be used carefully and after much consideration. The more interpersonal distance between two people talking, the less likely the conversation will end in agreement or satisfaction for both parties. People in this culture stand and sit very closely as they converse in order to better understand each others' "true" self.

After students have read or heard the conversation, ask them to consider some of the following questions in small groups or as a large class: How did you perceive each culture? Which cultural way of engaging in conversation do you most identify with and why? Which characteristics of each culture comprise your own conversational style? What difficulties might arise when people from these two cultures attempt to engage in conversation? What can people do to prevent these difficulties? Think of an intercultural conversation that you engaged in that included some of the nonverbal differences between Culture A and B. How did you deal with the differences then and would you deal differently with them now?

Exercise 5.6: Understanding Unfamiliar Cues. Just as with spoken language, we can oftentimes not understand a nonverbal message that another person has sent us. Although these confusing nonverbal messages can take place during intracultural or intercultural communication situations, they can be especially confusing during intercultural interactions because there is often very little shared understanding among participants. For example, it is common among Kenyans to summon another person by making a forceful "tsss tsss" sound. To a culturally different visitor this can sound very much like calling an animal instead of a human being because it is similar to whistling when calling a dog in the U.S. In addition, this sound is made when getting the attention of both animals and people in Kenya. What is a visitor supposed to make of such a nonverbal message? Should offense be taken or understood as merely a pragmatic way of summoning a person with whom you wish to speak?

The following exercise asks students to consider nonverbal messages that they have found confusing during interactions with people from cultures different from their own. Ask students to answer each of the questions below in small groups. They should reflect on the nonverbal messages that they have experienced that left them feeling a bit confused or even offended. Each group should try to come up with at least two examples for questions one through three. Ask each group to share their responses with the class.

1. What are some nonverbal messages that can often cause confusion among people who are relatively culturally similar?
2. What are some nonverbal messages that can often cause confusion among people who do not share the same cultural background? Use your own experience to respond to this question.
3. Think about a conversation during which you did not completely understand some nonverbal messages that were being sent. Describe the conversation and the confusing nonverbal message(s).
4. At the time, what did you think this message meant? How did you arrive at this interpretation?
5. Could some kind of cultural difference account for your confusion? Why or why not?
6. How did the message and your confusion affect the outcome of the conversation or relationship?

Exercise 5.7: An Experiment in Gender and Nonverbal Communication. Have students choose a gender-specific, nonverbal interactional rule from the article by Borisoff and Merrill, and systematically break the rule for two to three days. During the time of the experiment, students should keep detailed records of others' reactions, as well as their own feelings about and difficulties with the experiment. Inform students that they will be expected to type up and turn in a brief written report of their findings and reflections modeled on the outline provided below. Be sure the students know that they are also expected to complete and turn in answers to the questions listed under "preparation."

During the next class period, invite volunteers to share stories about what happened to them during the experiment. You may also wish to go through the discussion questions listed below as a group. Caution students that they should not engage in behavior that would make someone very uncomfortable, jeopardize a relationship, or even hurt themselves or another person. These kinds of informal experiments should first *do no harm*. As a precaution, it is wise for teachers to review all chosen rules before students set out to break them.

Outline for the Experiment

I.   Gender-specific, nonverbal rule:
II.   How I will attempt to break the rule:
III. Hypothesis:
IV.   Observations:
V.   Reflections:
VI.   Conclusions:
      (questions for class discussion):
      1.   Was this experiment relatively easy or difficult to carry out? Why?
      2.   Were you surprised by others' reactions to your infraction of the rules or did they do exactly what you expected?
      3.   Before this experiment, did you believe that our nonverbal behaviors reflect the power dynamics of our society? Why or why not?
      4.   Do you believe this now, after the experiment? Why or why not?
      5.   Do you feel you learned from this experiment and if so what did you learn?
      6.   As a culture, which nonverbal communication behaviors discussed by the authors must we challenge first? Why are these most significant?
      7.   How could we challenge and begin to change these dynamics? Give concrete examples.
      8.   Do you feel this experiment is itself a challenge to cultural norms? Is it a significant challenge? Why or why not? If not, what would have made it more significant? Can you think of other ways to challenge scripted gender roles in nonverbal behavior?
      9.   As an individual, is there something in particular that you want to change about your own nonverbal communication behaviors? Why? How will you accomplish this?

Test Items for Chapter 5

Multiple Choice

1.   Nonverbal behaviors that consist of body movements, gestures, and facial expressions are categorized as
      a.   chronemics.
      b.   proxemics.
      c.   kinesics. *
      d.   paralanguage.

2.   Differences between Arab cultures in which people tend to stand closely together when speaking and North American cultures in which people carry on conversation at a distance of eighteen to thirty-six inches are differences in
     a.   olfactics.
     b.   vocalics.
     c.   haptics.
     d.   proxemics. *

3.   Nonverbal behaviors that communicate warmth and closeness are referred to as _____ behaviors.
     a.   contact
     b.   immediacy *
     c.   collective
     d.   internal

4.   Cultures that display a high degree of "expressive" behaviors have been labeled as
     a.   high-contact cultures. *
     b.   masculine.
     c.   interdependent.
     d.   individualistic cultures.

5.   In a low-context culture, most of the information is contained within
     a.   the physical context of the message.
     b.   the person sending a message.
     c.   the person receiving a message.
     d.   the explicit message itself. *

6.   According to McDaniel, which cultural trait lessens Japanese reliance on verbal exchange?
     a.   vague statements
     b.   empathy *
     c.   ambiguity in conversations
     d.   None of the above

7.   Hand gestures are never used in Japan in reference to a person who is present at the time because
     a.   it is against Confucian ethics.
     b.   the Japanese do not use any nonverbal gestures.
     c.   this reduces the opportunity for offending anyone present and sustains harmony. *
     d.   none of the above

8.   By avoiding eye contact, Japanese participants
     a.   evince an air of humility and sustain *wa*. *
     b.   exercise power.
     c.   indicate disagreement.
     d.   none of the above

9.	The Japanese attitude toward personal space is contradictory because
	a.	they are passive about personal space but active about office space.
	b.	in uncrowded situations they maintain their personal space, but in crowded situations they do not resist contact with strangers. *
	c.	they strive to maintain greater personal space with Americans but less personal space with Hispanics.
	d.	none of the above

10.	The Japanese proclivity for conservative dress styles and colors emphasizes their value of
	a.	proper dress.
	b.	status.
	c.	collectivism. *
	d.	all of the above

11.	Monochronic time is characterized by
	a.	doing several tasks at once.
	b.	the need for a strong leader.
	c.	doing one thing at a time. *
	d.	the lack of a large bureaucracy.

12.	Polychronic time is characterized by
	a.	keeping a tight schedule.
	b.	the possibility that plans may need to be changed at the last minute. *
	c.	not being on time for appointments.
	d.	individuals having little knowledge of each other's activities.

13.	Hall concludes about P-time and M-time that
	a.	P-time is superior to M-time.
	b.	M-time has more advantages than P-time.
	c.	P-time users cannot learn to understand M-time.
	d.	P-time and M-time do not mix. *

14.	According to Judith Butler (1990), gender
	a.	is a chosen set of acts and social performances.
	b.	is produced through a stylization of the body. *
	c.	corresponds to a unique speech community.
	d.	all of the above

15.	According to Borisoff and Merrill, which of the following are shaped by cultural values and expectations?
	a.	physical build
	b.	gendered communication styles
	c.	nonverbal interactions
	d.	all of the above *

16. As young American girls are learning to smile more, young American boys are learning
    a.   to frown more.
    b.   to be more expressive.
    c.   to be less expressive. *
    d.   to look while listening.

17. Women's greater facility with decoding nonverbal messages has been attributed to
    a.   the needs of their subordinate status.
    b.   their greater tendency toward affiliation.
    c.   their moral superiority.
    d.   a & b *

True/False

T	1.	Nonverbal messages tell us how to interpret verbal messages.
T	2.	The most externally obvious code of nonverbal behavior is physical appearance.
T	3.	The nonverbal elements of the voice is known as paralanguage.
F	4.	High Context cultures rely less on nonverbal communication and more on verbal communication.
T	5.	High Context cultures are also somewhat more collectivistic and less individualistic than low context cultures.
T	6.	Smiling, Touching, eye contact, closer distances, and more vocal animation are examples of immediacy behaviors.
F	7.	More countries are more masculine (that is, competitive and assertive).
F	8.	People typically make conscious choices about their nonverbal behavior.
T	9.	Nonverbal communication is subject to cultural variation.
F	10.	When confronted with out-group members, Japanese can be quite expressive and display considerable nonverbal affiliativeness.
T	11.	Self-restraint of body movement in out-group environments by the Japanese is designed to avoid attention and maintain situational harmony or balance.
F	12.	Japanese children experience little touch from their mothers and this non-touch standard continues into adulthood.
T	13.	For the Japanese, laughter can signal joy, disguise embarrassment, sadness, and anger.
F	14.	P-time and M-time are the same across cultures.
T	15.	Members of typically polychronic time cultures can adapt to monochromic time.
T	16.	In contemporary America, women are still socialized to take up less space.
F	17.	Within same-sex dyads, men are usually much freer than women to touch one another.
F	18.	On average, men are more facially expressive than women.
F	19.	Borisoff and Merrill believe that men take up more physical space than women because of their biological drive to dominate.

Essay Questions

1. Andersen claims that "culture is primarily a nonverbal phenomenon." How does he support his argument?
2. Differentiate between individualism and collectivism as they refer to dimensions of nonverbal communication and culture.
3. What does Andersen mean when he indicates that some cultures are masculine while others are feminine?
4. What accounts for the finding that in individualistic countries like the United States, small talk, flirting, and dating are more important than in more collectivist cultures?
5. Referring to at least two different articles, differentiate between high- and low-context cultures.
6. Explain how social balance affects nearly all Japanese nonverbal behavior.
7. What does McDaniel mean by the "thematic consistency concept" in regard to culture?
8. Differentiate between Hall's conceptions of monochromic and polychronic time. In your discussion, provide specific examples of each.
9. Identify two advantages and two disadvantages of monochromic time.
10. Identify two advantages and two disadvantages of polychronic time.
11. What is the relationship between gender and perception of time?
12. What is the relationship between high- and low-context cultures and M-time and P-time?
13. When communicating interculturally, why would it be important to take into consideration both intentional and unintentional forms of nonverbal communication?
14. Borisoff and Merrill write: "In North American culture, space is a signifier of power, and individuals who have command over greater amounts of space and territory are often considered to have greater power" (269). Working from this statement, describe how space is used in an environment which you are familiar.
15. In your own words, write a definition of gender as Borisoff and Merrill understand it. Do you accept this definition? What is missing? How would you have defined gender before reading their article?

Chapter 6
Cultural Contexts: The Influence of the Setting

Chapter Synopsis

After reading this chapter, students will be more aware of the influence of culture on contexts such as small group communication in the workplace, discussion and negotiation strategies, counseling situations, health care, and the classroom. Students should be able to make connections between their own experiences of communicating within each of the contexts discussed in the readings and compare their own cultural expectations with those articulated by the authors. This chapter offers students some practical application of the concepts presented in the previous two chapters.

Quasha and McDaniel discuss how traditional Japanese modes of business communication will be jeopardized by the nation's economic push to become a global power in the information technology field. The article provides a historical overview of the formation of Japan's modern-day hierarchical structure. The effect of information technology on the Japanese corporate environment is also addressed. Lindsley and Braithwaite provide a brief overview of the problems that have arisen from business practices between Mexicans and Americans over the last ten years. They then discuss five core concepts of Mexican culture in order to alleviate miscommunication between Mexicans and Americans doing business in Mexico.

Brett provides a review of the literature on negotiation and culture. She discusses what occurs when cultures clash during negotiation and offers ideas for how cultural clash can be avoided. Rao provides a look into the interaction between physicians and patients. A review of the literature is provided on the impact of culture on physician-patient communication. Data is provided from interviews with physicians in Argentina, Brazil, and India.

The final article in this chapter explores cultural diversity in university classrooms. Because most university students will take some of their courses from instructors from different countries, students need to see the classroom as a multicultural, international environment. Gay offers insight and practical advice to students to assist them in navigating and learning in the diverse university classroom.

Discussion Ideas

1.   How did it make you feel to read Quasha and McDaniel's description of U.S. culture and values? Did some of you ever feel defensive about being compared to Japanese culture in these ways? Did anything in their description of the U.S. strike you as particularly accurate or completely wrong? How can we use their view as an opportunity to look at American culture from a different perspective?

2.   If you could take the best of Japanese and American business practices and create an entirely new business environment or culture, what would it look like? In other words, which elements from each culture would you adopt or discard? Is it even possible to combine individual elements in this way since the underlying cultural philosophies are so different? Does it make any sense? Are you able to generate a new cultural philosophy that represents a genuine blend of U.S. and Japanese cultures?

3.   Explain the Mexican notion of "face." How does the core concept of confianza relate to saving face? What about the concept of sympatia? Compare the Mexican understanding of "face" to the Japanese notion of "face" discussed by Quasha and McDaniel earlier in the chapter. What are the similarities? Differences?

4.   How would you define negotiation? Explain how direct confrontation is involved in negotiation. Explain how culture clash can occur during a negotiation. How can it be avoided?

5.   Discuss how culture might impact physician-patient communication.

6.   Discuss how culture plays a role in classroom communication. Ask students to draw upon their own experiences.

Exercises

Exercise 6.1: Classroom Visitors. This activity is designed to give students a much more in-depth understanding of the role that culture plays in the business, health care, and classroom contexts and applies to all the articles in this chapter. It allows students to listen to and ask questions of business professionals, health care providers, and teachers. Students will acquire some "real life" understanding of the consequences of culture in the realm of business. Further, students will gain insight into how interaction between patients and health care workers can be affected by different perceptions of how illness should be prevented and treated. Students will also be able to talk with teachers about how culture has an impact on the school classroom in the United States.

This activity can be accomplished in two ways. First, students can interview someone in the business, healthcare, or educational context, ask the questions below, and then report their findings to the class. A second option is for you to invite members from all three contexts to visit your classroom. Invite two or three business professionals to your class. These visitors can be contacted via personal affiliations, local business communities, or through businesses that have a partnership with your college or university, As your visitors to address changes in the business environment due to culture. How have the personal cultural demographics of the organization changed over the last five/ten years? What cultural sensitivity training is being done? What adaptations/accommodations have been made due to increased cultural diversity in the workplace? Have office arrangements, space, time usage, uniforms, etc. been altered? Negotiations? Group dynamics? What difficulties arise in the multicultural organization?

Next, invite two or three health care workers (nurses, doctors, public health workers, counselors, etc.) to your class. These visitors can be contacted on your college or university campus or from the surrounding community. Such health care facilities as Planned Parenthood, womencare and community clinics, hospices, local hospitals, and the health department in your city are excellent possible resources. Ask your visitors to address the role that culture and cultural sensitivity have in their jobs and share some of their experiences with their clients and patients who come from different cultures. What are some of the difficulties that they had to face? How are their intercultural interactions enjoyable and stimulating? What strategies do they use to help their clients? How successful are they? What suggestions do they have for improving relations between culturally different patients and health care workers?

Finally, invite two or three K-12 teachers to your class. These visitors can be contacted at local schools throughout your community. Invite teachers who teach in a multicultural school and who are culturally diverse among themselves. Other resources are the local school districts in your community. They may be able to direct you to individuals in charge of multicultural programs and multicultural specialists at certain schools. Ask your visitors to address the influence that culture has in the classroom and share some of the experiences they have had with their students. Ask them to describe the cultural backgrounds of their students and the different learning styles to which their students are accustomed. What are the specific needs of students who come from different cultures? What difficulties arise in a multicultural classroom? What aspects do they particularly enjoy and find rewarding? What strategies do they use to teach children from different cultures? How are non-English speaking students assisted in their school and classroom?

Invite students to ask the speakers questions. This activity can also be done with visitors from the business, health care, and education professions sharing the same class period. A debriefing session during the class session after the visits would be helpful to allow students to discuss some of their own thoughts about the visitors and the impact of culture on context. Possible questions for discussion: What are your own cross-cultural experiences in the business, health care or educational environment? Do you think our society addresses the issue of cultural differences in the business, healthcare, or classroom environment(s) enough? Give examples of how U.S. society has conceptualized and administered business, healthcare, and education from a mono-cultural perspective. Give examples of how U.S. society has attempted to adapt to cultural diversity in the business, healthcare, and educational settings. What type of training could you suggest for business professionals, health care providers, and educators to make them more aware of cultural differences and the need to be sensitive to these differences?

Exercise 6.2: Cultural Translation Simulation. This exercise is meant to accompany Quasha and McDaniel's article on cultural and communicative differences between Japanese and U.S. business environments. The activity treats Japanese and American cultural value systems as though they were two separate languages, playing on the notion of translation. In this way, the exercise makes literal the difficulty of intercultural communication. It suggests that even when everyone is speaking the same language (English for the purposes of this exercise), they are not necessarily "speaking the same language."

Get three volunteers to enact a business meeting between a Japanese executive, an American manager, and a "cultural translator." Both business people will be speaking in English for the purposes of the class, but each will adopt the verbal and nonverbal communication styles appropriate for their culture as described by Quasha and McDaniel. A third person who is familiar with the communication styles and values of both cultures will be stuck in the middle to act as cultural translator.

Explain to your three volunteers that this is an initial meeting between the two companies meant to initiate interaction and give each company the opportunity to make projections or plans about how the deal will be conducted. In other words, these two individuals might discuss: how long the deal should take, what the process will involve, the stages of negotiation, how much interaction should take place between the employees of the two companies, and the scheduling of future meetings. Inform students that there is a status differential between the two: the Japanese company is represented by the company president and the U.S. company is represented by an upper-middle manager.

Be sure to encourage the whole class to participate actively in the skit. If and when the translator gets completely stuck, have members of the class help out. Also, have students take notes on what they are seeing. At the end of the skit, ask the students to share their observations. Make sure to also give the volunteers a chance to tell the class what it was like to be in the various situations they found themselves in throughout the skit.

Activity 6.3: Cultural Views of Job Satisfaction. Different people may want different things from their intimate relationships with others. Some are looking for only basic companionship, others want someone who will listen and empathize, and still others are searching for a person who will primarily satisfy their physical needs for affection and sex. We can't assume that our partners want what we want from our relationship. The same notion holds true when we try to determine what people look for in their jobs and careers. While some people may be looking for stable, high-paying employment, others are primarily interested in working with co-workers who are supportive and friendly. And just as in our romantic relationships, if we assume that the people we work with seek the same kind of working conditions and environment that we do, our assumptions may result in crossed-signals and miscommunication.

This exercise asks students to identify the components of job satisfaction for themselves and then to ask someone who has a different cultural background to assess his or her needs as an employee. Because different cultures value and conceive of work differently, students may come up with some interesting contrasts. Ask students to rank the following items from 1 to 10 according to how important they feel each is in contributing to their morale as an employee. Then have them ask an acquaintance or friend who is from a different country or ethnic group to do the same for the second set of items. If you class is very diverse, students may wish to simply exchange and compare their responses with a member of the class. What differences do they see between the two sets of rankings? How might such differences affect working relationships?

Your Description of Job Satisfaction		Your Friend's Description of Job Satisfaction
_____	Interesting work	_____
_____	Personal loyalty of supervisors	_____
_____	Full appreciation of work done	_____
_____	Help on personal problems	_____
_____	High wages	_____
_____	Job Security	_____
_____	Tactful discipline	_____
_____	Feeling of being in on things	_____
_____	Good working conditions	_____
_____	Promotion in the company	_____

Pose some of the following questions to students in a class discussion: What differences do you see between the item you ranked as number one and the item your friend ranked as number one? What do you think accounts for these differences? What differences do you see between the item you ranked as number ten and the item your friend ranked as number ten? What do you think accounts for these differences?

Consider your ranking of the job satisfaction items. What do you feel has influenced this ranking? How might your culture, upbringing, experiences, beliefs, and values have affected your needs as an employee? Ask the friend who ranked the second list of items to consider how his or her culture, upbringing, experiences, beliefs, and values influenced his or her job needs. Consider the differences you found between the two sets of job satisfaction rankings. How might such differences affect the working relationship between two co-workers? How would each approach his or her job? How can we adapt to the different needs of our co-workers? As supervisors, how can we adapt to the different notions of job satisfaction of our employees?

Activity 6.4: Cultural Notions of Health and Illness. This exercise asks students to consider the following questions: How do health care workers perceive the communication process with their clients? Do they adapt their typical way of communicating when interacting with a client who is of the opposite sex, from a different country, or of a different ethnic group? The goal of this exercise is to find out how doctors, nurses, and health care professionals perceive and respond to the influence of culture in their interpersonal relationships with patients and clients. Ask students to contact two or three professionals in the health care field and talk with them for approximately thirty minutes about their interactions with patients who are in some way culturally dissimilar to themselves. These people can be contacted through medical school, nursing, and public health programs on most college or university campuses. Students can also contact health care professionals in their communities. Planned Parenthood, women's and community clinics, hospices, local hospitals, and the city health department are excellent resources.

Below is a list of questions for students to use to conduct their interviews. Add questions of your own to this list. Encourage students to send a copy of the questions they will be asking to the people they will interview before the day of the interview. This will give them an opportunity to reflect on their interactions with patients. After students have completed their interviews, ask them to respond to the six questions listed under "Post Interview Questions." Ask students to share their responses with their classmates by participating in small group discussions. They should pool their "data" and answer the following general questions: How does culture affect the health care setting and relationships between health care professionals and their clients? How does culture affect communication in these relationships?

Interview Questions

a. Describe some of the patients/clients that you see in your work.
b. Describe the cultural backgrounds of some of your patients.
c. How would you describe the relationship between a client or patient and a health care professional?
d. How does communication play a role in your treatment of a patient?

e. How is communication more challenging when the patient is from a different cultural background as your own?

f. What do you do to adapt to the patient's way of communicating?

g. Would you describe a situation when you found communication with a culturally different patient particularly challenging?

h. How has a patient's cultural beliefs about doctors and illness affected your communication with and subsequent treatment of this person?

Post Interview Questions

a. What health care professional did you interview and how many years experience does he or she have?

b. What is this person's cultural background?

c. How does this person describe the client-health care professional relationship?

d. What role does communication have in his or her treatment of a patient?

e. How do the cultural backgrounds of his or her patients affect interactions with them?

f. Have the particular cultural values and beliefs of a patient ever affected this health care professional's communication with or treatment of a patient?

Exercise 6.5: Diversity and Discussion in the Classroom. The classroom can be an excellent environment to engage in intercultural communication with people from a variety of backgrounds. Some of the most fruitful and compelling learning takes place in classes where students from all walks of life engage in discussions about issues that affect our world. Without such diversity, students would have only like-minded individuals to share their ideas with; debate and critical thinking are often stifled in such environments. The danger of fervent discussion among diverse peoples, however, is that such conversations can result in the breakdown of communication because views may be so different that no common ground appears to exist. How can diverse students engage in meaningful discussion and debate while building and maintaining interpersonal relationships that can survive beyond the classroom?

This exercise asks students to consider two classroom scenarios where university students are debating the often controversial issues of affirmative action and women's rights. In each hypothetical scenario, students from different cultural, ethnic, religious, and political backgrounds are gathered to discuss each of these issues. Ask students to read each scenario and respond to question that follows from the viewpoint of a student who is also taking part in the discussion. As members of this class, students should consider what they can do to encourage the development of a comprehensive, thought-provoking discussion. What interpersonal dynamics must be considered when opposing opinions may be couched in an antagonistic tone or based on strongly held cultural values?

Discussion #1
Affirmative Action

Students in "Policy Making in the United States" settle into their seats. The instructor begins the discussion on affirmative action by giving some historical background on what it is and why it was initially implemented. After this introduction, she asks students to express their views on the goals of affirmative action and whether they feel it is a policy that should continue. Jennifer, a Caucasian woman in her mid 20s, is the first to speak.

"I just don't think affirmative action is necessary anymore. At one point in time, like in the 60s, it was important to enable women and people of color to have equal access to all jobs and careers. But those opportunities are now available to all people, not just white males."

After Jennifer finishes, George, a Mexican American man of about 20, immediately responds to her comment.

"Things are not that different today. People of color don't have access to all jobs and careers because they must still face the racism and discrimination that often go on when they apply for a job."

"But why should you discriminate against whites in order not to discriminate against blacks? It doesn't make sense."

"Affirmative action is not about discrimination against whites. It's about making sure that people who have previously been left out of the game get a chance to play."

"What ever you want to call it, it really is discrimination--reverse discrimination."

"You can only see it for what it isn't doing for whites instead of seeing what it is doing to help nonwhites."

There is a momentary pause as George finishes. You raise your hand to make a comment. The teacher calls on you.

Question: Write out how you would respond to Jennifer and George's short dialogue. Consider not only your own opinions about affirmative action but perhaps more importantly, think about how you as a fellow discussant can contribute to the primary goal of the discussion: to exchange disparate opinions while encouraging positive interpersonal dynamics among diverse class members.

Discussion #2
Women's Rights

You are in an Anthropology 101 discussion section and the topic of the present unit is women's lives in developing countries. The teaching assistant in your class has begun a discussion on marriage customs in Islamic cultures of Africa. Hanan, a Muslim woman from Ethiopia, offers a comment.

"In some countries, it is common for Islamic children to be betrothed when they are very young, especially girls. Sometimes girls of eight or nine are betrothed to men in their twenties but they live with their parents until puberty."

Kathy, a woman born and raised in the U.S., immediately responds to Hanan. They begin a dialogue.

"O.K.., so it 's real common. But is it fair? I mean, the girls don't even have a say in who they will spend their lives with, who their husbands will be. That seems to take away the rights of the girl?"

"It's the kind of life that some Muslims understand and accept. It's just a different way of looking at marriage. And Islam isn't the only religion that practices this kind of arrangement."

"I understand. But it just seems to force women to do something that they have no say in, no voice."

There is a momentary pause as Kathy finishes. You raise your hand to make a comment. The teacher calls on you.

Question: Write out how you would respond to Raija and Kathy's short dialogue. Consider not only your own opinions about Islamic marriage customs but perhaps more importantly, think about how you as a fellow discussant can contribute to the primary goal of the discussion: to exchange disparate opinions while encouraging positive interpersonal dynamics among diverse class members.

Test Items for Chapter 6

Multiple Choice

1. Japan's early experience under Tokugawa rule instilled a continuing sense of
    a. collectivism
    b. group orientation
    c. hierarchy
    d. all of the above *

2. Which of the following do the Japanese try to avoid?
    a. face to face business meetings
    b. conflict *
    c. use of humor
    d. all of the above

3. The Japanese concept of *wa* is most commonly translated as
    a. harmony *
    b. balance
    c. formality
    d. group work

4. Which of the following is seen as something that carries the potential to erode
    Japanese corporate hierarchies?
    a. written memos
    b. email *
    c. two hour lunches
    d. all of the above

5. Which of the following traditional Japanese modes of business communication
    will be jeopardized by the nation's economic push to become a global power
    in the IT field?
    a. decision making
    b. face-to-face meetings
    c. corporate structures
    d. all of the above *

6. The integration of which of the following has created a distinct form of business
    communication in Japan?
    a. collectivism, hierarchy, formality, face, and social stability *
    b. collectivism, hierarchy, formality, face, and power
    c. collectivism, hierarchy, formality, and face
    d. none of the above

7. Which of the following concepts for doing business in Mexico focuses on "trust"?
   a. confianza *
   b. simpatia
   c. palanca
   d. estabilidad

8. Which of the following core concepts for doing business in Mexico refers to the power derived from affiliated connections?
   a. confianza
   b. simpatia
   c. palanca *
   d. estabilidad

9. Which of the following core concepts for doing business in Mexico reinforces the value of personal relationships?
   a. confianza
   b. simpatia
   c. palanca
   d. estabilidad *

10. The value Mexicans place on stability or estabilidad is centered in
    a. the Catholic church.
    b. corporate affiliations.
    c. the government.
    d. the family. *

11. For Americans, "tomorrow" refers specifically to the following day, whereas for Mexicans, manana means which of the following?
    a. some time in the near future
    b. some time in the future that is always deferred
    c. some time in the future that may be deferred *
    d. a & c

12. During financial hardships an employee might continue to work for his or her manager without a paycheck. Which core concept does this demonstrate?
    a. confianza
    b. simpatia
    c. palanca
    d. establidad *

13. Which of the following is true about BATNAs?
    a. they are not fixed
    b. they are frequently unrelated
    c. one party may be able to impose its BATNA on the other
    d. all of the above are true about BATNA's *

14. With information about relative power a negotiator can judge which of the following?
    a. when to walk away from an negotiation with confidence
    b. when to press for more in a negotiation
    c. when to accept an offer
    d. all of the above *

15. Which of the following set high personal goals in negotiation?
    a. individualists *
    b. collecitvists
    c. both a and b
    d. none of the above

16. In hierarchical cultures which of the following is true?
    a. social superiors are granted power and privilege
    b. social inferiors are obligated to defer to social superiors
    c. social superiors are have an obligation to look out for the needs of social inferiors
    d. all of that above are true *

17. A "half-truth" can be defined as
    a. physicians who did not disclose a diagnosis immediately
    b. physicians who described the diagnosis in doses over several visits
    c. physicians who informed a family member of the diagnosis before telling the patient
    d. all of the above can be defined as "half-truths" *

18. Which of the following is an individualistic culture?
    a. Argentina
    b. Brazil
    c. India
    d. United States *

19. Participatory-interactive communication style has been observed among
    a. African Americans
    b. Latinos
    c. Native Hawaiians
    d. all of the above *

20. Which of the following uses "talk story" to create an idea, tell a story, or complete a learning task?
    a. Native Hawaiian students *
    b. Asian students
    c. European American students
    d. African American students

21. Who employs "topic-chaining" discourse as a way to communicate in the classroom?
    a. African American students *
    b. Asian students
    c. Native American students
    d. none of the above

22. Through which of the following ways do African Americans "gain the floor" or get participatory entry into conversations?
    a. personal assertiveness
    b. the strength of the impulse to be involved
    c. the persuasive power of the point they wish to make
    d. all of the above *

True/False

T   1. The Japanese use periods of silence to show disagreement without actually saying so directly.

T   2. Due to different cultural understandings of conflict management and negotiation, Americans often underestimate the time it will take to negotiate a business deal with a Japanese company.

F   3. The traditional Japanese approach to management will work will in an IT environment.

F   4. NAFTA has helped small businesses in the U.S., Canada, and Mexico.

F   5. U.S. plants located south of the border have been praised for providing a good wage, keeping their workers healthy and safe, and respecting following environmental policy.

F   6. Planca refers to paying a bribe.

T   7. Americans have a tendency to think about manana as referring to some specific time period.

F   8. In a study by Tinsley and Brett (1998) they discovered that during a 45 minute negotiation, Hong Kong Chinese negotiators resolved more issues than were the U.S. negotiators.

F   9. When negotiators are from different cultures their negotiation strategies invariably clash.

F   10. Western medical training programs are actively integrating intercultural communication training in their curriculum.

T   11. The task of understanding and diagnosing medical conditions is often complicated by cultural differences.

T   12. Interaction between a physician and patient is inherently an intercultural encounter even when the two parties perceive they are from the same culture.

F   13. "Yes" always means yes across cultural boundaries.

T	14.	Most Argentinean physicians focused primarily on education and socioeconomic status to describe the diversity in their country.
T	15.	Physicians in Argentina, Brazil, and India saw their countries as hetereogeneous.
T	16.	Among African Americans the *participatory-interactive* style of communicating is sometimes referred to as *call-response*.
T	17.	African Americans "gain the floor" or get participatory entry into conversations through personal assertiveness.
T	18.	The most common practice among teachers is to ask convergent questions and use deductive approaches to solving problems.
F	19.	The gender of a person communicating may be more problematic than the "gendered" style of communication.
T	20.	Students of color who are strongly affiliated with their traditional cultures tend to be more inductive, interactive, and communal in task performance.
F	21.	In traditional African American and Latino cultures, problem solving in not contextual.
T	22.	African Americans engage in the participatory-interactive style of communicating.
T	23.	Latinos engage in the participatory-interactive style of communicating.

Essay Questions

1. Discuss the arrangement of Japanese business offices versus those in the United States. How do these arrangements affect communication in Japan and the United States?
2. Explain the *sempai-kohai* relationship in Japanese culture. How does this relationship affect communication in Japanese companies?
3. How will traditional Japanese modes of business communication be affected by the information technology field? Provide specific examples to substantiate your response.
4. Briefly describe the difference between how Americans and Mexicans begin a business meeting. What is the cultural significance of these different approaches?
5. Explain Mexican core concept of simpatia. How might an American misunderstand this concept? What is it about American cultural values that would make for such misunderstandings?
6. Americans often find the practices surrounding palanca to be corrupt without reflecting on similar practices common in the U.S. What are some of the American business practices that are comparable? Use concrete examples and explain your answer.
7. Discuss the concept of time in Mexican business. Include in your discussion the meaning of *manana* in Mexico versus how Americans view this concept. Provide examples to support your response.
8. Discuss the concept of *estabilidad* in the Mexican work environment.

9.   Discuss *compradrazgo* and *comadrazgo* systems as a way for managers to demonstrate responsibility for employees' well-being.

10.   What are distributive and integrative agreements? What is the potential for integrative agreements?

11.   Discuss conflict within hierarchical cultures and egalitarian cultures.

12.   How does being from an individualist culture impact negotiation? How does being from an collectivist culture impact negotiation?

13.   Review the concept of BATNA as it relates to egalitarian and hierarchical cultures.

14.   Provide suggestions for what can be done to avoid culture clashes in negotiation.

15.   What strategies can be taken to avoid culture clashes in negotiation. Be specific with your response.

16.   How can culture inhibit physician-patient communication? Provide specific examples for support.

17.   Explain the concept of half-truths in physician-patient communication. How does this concept relate to collectivism?

18.   Explain how physicians perceptions of cultural diversity in Argentina and Brazil differ from those in India.

19.   How do physicians define success in terms of their interaction with patients?

20.   How can culturally-determined rules dictating what is appropriate content for communication influence teaching and learning in university classrooms?

21.   Differentiate between passive-receptive and participatory-interactive styles of discourse.

22.   Discuss some of the reasons why Asian Americans perform so well in high-level mathematics classes. Could these same reasons be adapted to other ethnic groups, i.e., African Americans. If so, why? If not, why not?

23.   Discuss some traditional women's ways of communicating and how they can be problematic to classroom teachers.

24.   Discuss topic-centered and topic-associated or topic-chaining techniques as forms of discourse in a classroom.

Chapter References

Powell, B. (1995, November 6), Keep your profits, Newsweek, p.98.

Mullavey-O'Byrne, C. (1994). Intercultural Communication for Health Care Professionals. In R. W. Brislin & T. Yoshida, (Eds.), Improving Intercultural Interaction: Modules for Cross-Cultural Training Programs. London: Sage Publications.

Part 4
Intercultural Communication: Seeking Improvement

Chapter 7
Communicating Interculturally: Becoming Competent

Chapter Synopsis

Chapter 7 represents a shift in the orientation of the *Reader* from raising awareness of similarities and differences between and across cultures toward practical advice for communicating interculturally. Articles in this chapter address both problems and solutions in a variety of intercultural contexts. Descriptions of and suggestions for competent communication interculturally are offered. After reading this chapter, students should be more prepared to actually engage in intercultural communication rather than simply talk about it.

In the first essay, Chen and Starosta stress the importance of intercultural awareness. Three levels of intercultural awareness are addressed along with two approaches of for the study of intercultural awareness. Baldwin and Hecht discuss identity and intolerance. They focus on the dynamics between African Americans and White Americans and address seven issues that important to African Americans as they interact with White Americans. After reading this article students should be able to more aware of their own identity and ways to address intolerance. Mak, Westwood, Ishimaya, and Barker address the many benefits immigrants can obtain from learning skills of intercultural competence. Psychological barriers to developing these skills are discussed.

Ting-Toomey focuses on the specific context of intercultural conflict. Her essay offers students a framework within which to understand cultural differences in the event of interpersonal conflict, but also suggests a series of skills that can be helpful in managing conflict when it occurs in the intercultural encounter. Sauceda shares some of his experiences as a co-cultural mediator and offers some of the strategies he believes to be effective in his role as a mediator. Conflicts in Police/Community relations, mental health services, the workplace, and the educational setting are provided as ways for the reader to understand the strategies he offers for becoming effective intercultural communicators with people from various co-cultures.

Begley examines the phenomenon of cultural adaptation by providing answers to the following question, "What does one face when one crosses cultural boundaries?" She helps us not only understand the phenomenon of *culture shock*, but provides us with ideas for adapting successfully to a new cultural environment. Finally Collier's article provides a series of ten questions to help students think critically about intercultural interactions. She encourages students to focus on the processes by which people construct their cultural identities. Perhaps most importantly, this article helps to establish a conceptual foundation for students' reading, thinking, and perceptive practices that they have experienced.

Discussion Ideas

1. What are the six components of intercultural sensitivity according to Chen and Starosta? How does each of these relate to intercultural sensitivity as they define it?

2. What is the relationship between low- and high-context cultures and cultures that are primarily individualistic or collectivistic with regard to approaches to conflict? Differentiate between the role of third-party intervention in individualistic, low-context cultures and collectivistic high-context cultures. Why would it be important in a high context culture to have an impartial mediator?

3. Sauceda suggests that we "Teach Transcendence" rather than "Teach Tolerance". What does he mean by this suggestion? How can we teach "transcendence"?

4. Begley suggests that cross-cultural adaptation encompasses such experiences as culture shock, assimilation, adjustment, acculturation, integration, and coping. How do these terms differ? Begley also identifies several challenges to cross-cultural adaptation, such as ethnocentrism, differences in language, disequilibrium, and length of stay. Of course, not all cross-cultural situations offer the same level of adaptation difficulties to sojourners. Consider the adaptation challenges that the refugees from Kosovo faced when they were forced from their homes in April, 1999, compared to those challenges faced by U.S. Peace Corps volunteers. How do the challenges described by Begley change when one *chooses* to cross over into another society versus people who are *forced* from their homes? What other challenges would you add to Begley's list to encompass forced cross-cultural adaptation?

5. What does it mean to have an individual identity? What does it mean to have a cultural identity? How do these two things differ? Are they interrelated, interconnected? This discussion can illuminate the connection between who we are as individuals and our culture.

    A. Ask students to identify five or six words that they feel best describe their personality.
    B. Then ask them to try to link these characteristics to one or more of the cultures with which they identify. Do they see any connections? Has their culture influenced the development of their self? If, for example, students say that they are friendly, would they also say that that friendliness is important to their culture?
    C. Trying to link their self and their culture will be a challenging task for many students, and in many instances students will have purposefully taken on personality characteristics that are not upheld by the teachings of their culture.
        These revelations will also be important because there may be specific reasons why they did not wish to adopt certain cultural characteristics.

6.   With which cultures do you identify? Why these and not others? Where are your primary loyalties? That is, what cultural characteristics do you adhere to most strongly? Are there some that may be more representative or one culture than another? This discussion can help students define cultural identity and question why they connect more with one cultural identity than another. Students can discover that who they are is often a combination of membership in many cultural groups. They should consider their religion, race, gender, sexual orientation, age, etc. when discussing these questions.

Exercises

Exercise 7.1: Improving Ourselves. This activity incorporates all of the articles in Chapter 7 and focuses on the communicative behavior of students and, specifically, those aspects of their behavior that they would like to change. This activity uses the concepts in the articles in Chapter 7 as a backdrop (competence, conflict, work force diversity, acculturation, and intercultural sensitivity) for improving intercultural communication. Using the articles in Chapter 7 as a starting point, students will be given an opportunity to verbalize and develop strategies for a particular characteristic of their communicative behavior that they view as a weakness or "problem area." Begin by asking students to come prepared for the next class period with one aspect of their communicative behavior that they see as problematic or that needs "fixing." Encourage them to talk to their friends or family and solicit their opinions. But the students must agree with their opinions since there is a tendency for people not to make an effort to change if they don't see a problem. Have students answer the following questions
1.   Describe this communicative behavior that you would like to change.
2.   Give one example when you communicated in this way. Include the other interactant's response to your behavior.
3.   What strategy can you think of that will remedy this behavior?

When students come to the following class period, ask them to break into small groups. Each group member should share what they have written, ask the group for feedback about the strategy developed, and solicit other possible strategies. Each student should walk away from his or her group with a list of strategies. Regroup as a class and have students share some of their areas for change. The instructor should act as a probing questioner: What can you do to improve your communication with others? What will you do? How will you know if you have been successful? What affect will this improvement have on your relationships with other people?

Engage the class in a discussion on how their specific communication problems might affect their ability to be competent intercultural communicators. How might their behavior be perceived by individuals from other cultures? How would working on this one communicative behavior enhance their effectiveness as intercultural communicators? Hopefully the discussion will begin to address the issue of becoming interculturally competent through improving one's own communication with others. Encourage students to use some of the strategies offered. An assignment could even be given that asks them to document their attempts at actively applying one or more strategies.

Exercise 7.2: Intercultural Interviews.   Many of us may have grown up learning that you never ask a person how much salary he or she makes. Even among close friends, such a question may be considered highly inappropriate and suspicious. In cultures that believe money is sacred, a personal issue, and an indication of one's worth as an individual, such a question might be perceived as too face threatening and private. We learn from culture what we can ask certain people and what is generally perceived as taboo topics of conversation. Such norms are very culture-specific and breaking or following them can influence the development of intercultural friendships.

This exercise will help students explore what different cultures feel is appropriate and inappropriate to discuss as well as appropriate versus effective. Ask students to interview a friend, acquaintance, or classmate who does not share their cultural background. Below is a list of suggested interview questions. Students should explain that they are interested in finding out about culturally appropriate self-disclosing behavior and that he or she may stop the interview at any time. They should let their interviewees know that it is not their intent to pry into their personal lives but rather to learn from them what they feel are appropriate topics of conversation. Their goals should be made very explicit. Afterward, students should ask this person how she or he felt during the interview. Were certain questions too personal? Is it considered appropriate in this person's culture to talk about certain topics and not others?

Interview Questions

1. What is your academic major?
2. In what year of school are you?
3. What kind of music do you like?
4. What are your favorite foods?
5. What are some of your hobbies?
6. What is your impression of the university or college?
7. What country are you from or of which culture are you a member?
8. How would you describe your political beliefs (i.e., conservative, liberal, radical, etc.)?
9. How many family members do you have?
10. How would you describe your family?
11. Whom do you most admire?
12. What do you feel are the characteristics of a good friend?
13. What religion are you?
14. What is the most important thing in the world to you?
15. What do you think you will be doing five years from now?
16. How do you feel about your socioeconomic status?
17. When was the happiest moment in your life?
18. When was the unhappiest moment in your life?
19. What is one mistake you have made in your life?
20. What health problems do you have?

Post-interview Questions

Questions for the informant
1. Which questions did you not feel comfortable answering? Why?
2. Which questions would be most appropriate between people who are meeting for the first time? Between close friends? Among family members? Among romantic partners?
3. What topics do people in your culture always consider taboo in any contexts What topics are considered inappropriate for discussion with certain people or in certain situations?

Questions for the students to ask themselves
1. Which questions did you feel it was inappropriate to ask this person?
2. Was there any time during the interview when you perceived the other person feeling uncomfortable? Describe what you perceived.
3. How did you respond to this person's discomfort?
4. Describe a time when you obviously broke a conversational norm unintentionally. What happened and how did culture play a role?

Exercise 7.3: Developing Intercultural Relationships. This exercise accompanies the article by Chen and Starosta.   At times the unfamiliar can excite us. If we knew everything about the people we formed relationships with, there would be no surprises, nothing to uncover and explore. But too much unfamiliarity can be unsettling. We like to have something we can be certain of in our relationships. At least in the initial stages, intercultural relationships may be characterized by more uncertainty than intracultural relationships. This increased uncertainty about who another is might be one reason why people are sometimes hesitant to form relationships with culturally dissimilar individuals.

This exercise focuses on how we develop intercultural relationships and the attributes necessary for the development of such relationships. It asks students to consider their own network of friends and the extent to which they have developed relationships with people who are culturally dissimilar. First, ask students to respond to questions one and two below by themselves. Then have them get into small groups and respond to questions three through seven. As students answer each of the questions, they should consider their own intercultural relationships they have developed. Have each group report out some of their findings to the class.

Questions to Answer Individually

1.   How many relationships (romantic partners and people you consider to be friends) with culturally different people do you have? (Remember to consider relationships with people from different ethnicities, religions, sexual orientations, degree of able-bodiedness, sex, etc.) What types of relationships are these (i.e., friends, romantic partners, relatives, acquaintances, etc.) Discuss some possible reasons for the network of friends you have developed.
2.   Describe an intercultural relationship that you have with someone that you find to be very satisfying. What makes it so satisfying?

Questions to Answer in Small Groups

1.   List five positive and unique aspects of intercultural relationships.
2.   List five reasons why people are hesitant to develop relationships (platonic or romantic) with people from other cultures.
3.   Which one of the above reasons pertains (if at all) most directly to you? Please explain your answer.
4.   Many intercultural communication specialists mention open-mindedness as one attribute necessary for the development of successful intercultural relationships. What are some other attributes or ways of thinking that a person should have in order to develop relationships with culturally different people?
5.   Which of the above do you feel you might need to develop further? Why did you choose these attributes to work on?

Exercise 7.4: Individualism, Collectivism, Reward Distribution and Conflict. This activity can be used with Ting-Toomey's article on managing intercultural conflicts effectively. One area that may result in intercultural conflict is the area of reward distribution particularly when both collectivistic and individualist cultures are involved. Ting-Toomey notes:

> In terms of the relationship between the norm of fairness and cross-cultural conflict interaction style, results from past research indicate that individualists typically prefer to use the equity norm (self-deservingness norm) in dealing with reward allocation in group conflict interaction. In comparison, collectivists oftentimes prefer to use the equality norm (the equal distribution norm) to deal with in-group members and thus avoid group disharmony. (p. 379-380)

The following exercise was developed by R. W. Brislin (1994) and can be found in Improving Intercultural Interactions: Modules for Cross-cultural Training. Consult this excellent reference book for other appropriate exercises. Divide the students into two group (one group will represent collectivists and the other will represent individualists) and have the students read the case study on the next page. After reading the case study have each group draft up a distribution of money based on either their collectivist or individualists tendencies. Then have the groups role play a negotiation to resolve their distribution differences utilizing the conflict management strategies offered by Ting-Toomey.

For discussion, Brislin (1994) provides the following explanation to accompany the exercise:

> Individualists generally prefer an equity distribution, that is rewards based on contributions. If person A contributed 40% of the work he should receive approximately 40% of the rewards. Other people should also receive rewards based on their contributions. Person E is not likely to get much special attention from individualists in monetary terms. Instead, they might name the road after this high status person. Person F, despite his special circumstances would likely receive a share equal to his contributions. These distributions are based on the idea that it is necessary to reward individual accomplishment or the person will see little reason to work hard on the next project. In comparison, collectivists prefer an equality distribution in which all people receive the same level of rewards. If there were five people who contributed to the project, each would receive approximately 20% of the rewards. This will keep the group functioning smoothly. The idea is that if one person gets more, it will disrupt the group. Besides the lesser contributors may contribute more on the next project. Collectivists are also more likely to give special attention to person E whose status was instrumental in acquiring the project. They are likely to vote a solid $10,000 to person E in recognition of his effort even though he does not need the money. For person F with special circumstances, they are likely to give him more than the others in the group, or to assume that person F's special needs have already been taken care of by the company separate from the distribution of the $100,000. (pp. 80-81)

<u>Activity 7.4: Rewards Case Study (Brislin, 1994, pp. 80-81)</u>

Assume that you are employed in a company (for profit) that contracts to do construction work (e.g., roads, sewage treatment facilities) in rural areas of the community where you live. The company recently received a contract for $800,000 dollars (U.S.) to build a road. Given a number of fortunate circumstances, such as good weather, the project was completed for $700,000. It is now the end of the fiscal year and the board of directors has decided that the extra $100,000 can be distributed the way people (who were involved in the road construction project) decide. The following people are somehow involved. All have been in the company for at least five years and get along well together

Person A was the hardest worker and was clearly responsible for supervising a great deal of the actual day-to-day work on the project. At least 40% of the day-to-day work on the project was done by him. Persons B, C, and D were solid but not spectacular contributors. They were competent workers but not outstanding. Each contributed about 15% of the actual day-to-day work on the project. Person E is a very high status and wealthy person in the organization and in the community. Although he did not engage in any of day-to-day work on the road construction project and did not write the proposal for funding, it is known within the organization that he called upon his connections and used his influence so that the original $800,000 contract would go to the company.

Person F is a contributor much like B, C, and D. His contribution was about 15% of the work needed for the project's completion. M's father died recently, however, and person F has considerable expenses associated with the funeral, nursing care for his mother, and the education of his much younger brothers (his father left no estate).

Your group is unassociated with the project but has been asked to help in the decision making concerning the distribution of the $100,000. How would you distribute the money?

	Amount	**Explanation (Why?)**
Person A		
Person B		
Person C		
Person D		
Person E		
Person F		

Total = $100,000

Exercise 7.5: Acculturation. This activity is related to Begley's article on sojourner adaptation and will allow students to experience vicariously the process of acculturation. Using the information provided by Begley, students are to interview someone who has crossed cultural boundaries by entering the U.S. Depending on the diversity of the class, some students may be in the midst of the adaptation/acculturation process themselves. If so, these students may share their own personal experiences or they may choose to interview someone else. The idea is to make real for the students the dramatic and all-encompassing challenges of having to construct a new life in an unfamiliar place. Some of the following questions may be helpful when conducting the interview.

1. What things have you done to help deal with the high level of uncertainty and anxiety in moving to a new culture?
2. What cross-cultural challenges have you faced since moving to the U.S.?
3. Do you feel that your adaptation has been slow?
4. What do you miss most about your original culture?
5. Do you participate in a variety of social functions in the U.S.?
6. Are you in close contact with members of your own ethnicity here in the U.S.? How large is this group?
7. Do you maintain ties with your original culture? How often?
8. Do you feel the U.S. culture has been receptive and welcoming?
9. Do you feel pressure to conform to U.S. values, attitudes and beliefs?
10. Do you speak English? Has this influenced your adaptation to the culture?
11. What changes have occurred in you as a person as a result of your moving here?
12. Do you feel these are positive changes?

Exercise 7.6: Intercultural Talk Journals. In order to understand how people from other cultures communicate interpersonally, it is useful to actually engage in conversations with them. But talking is only the first step. Having students actively reflecting on their experiences with culturally different people can help them make sense of what happened, allow them to assess what they have learned, and make changes in their communication. This activity is designed to give students more intercultural experiences and familiarity with other cultures.

Ask students to start a "talk" journal during the first weeks of the term. In this journal, they should describe the interactions they have with people from different cultures and record some of their perceptions and feelings experienced during these encounters. Students should be reminded that although people may share their ethnic background, they may also be members of other cultures. Women, gays and lesbians, people who are deaf or blind, physically challenged individuals, Jews, Mormons, and the elderly are just a sampling of individuals who belong to cultures that have their own distinct way of living and orientation to the world. Writing in their talk journals about conversations with members of these cultures would be very appropriate (unless they themselves are members of these cultures).

Encourage students to write in their journals at the end of every week. Their comments and observations should focus on some of the topics listed below. You may wish to collect the journals and respond to some of the students' comments. Be aware, however, that knowing you will be reading their journals may alter students' entries; some students may not even wish you to read their entries. After students have made several entries in their talk journals, ask them to answer the questions entitled "Post Talk Journal Questions." Have students share (if they wish) their talk journal entrees and what they learned from them in a small group or class discussion towards the end of the quarter.

Suggested Topics for Talk Journal Entries

1. The number of interpersonal contacts with people from cultures different from your own.
2. Where did you encounter people from different cultures?
3. Descriptions of the encounters.
4. How do the people you spoke with communicate? What is important in their lives?
5. How is their culture manifested in their behavior or communication?
6. Were your interpersonal contacts marked by any misunderstandings due to cultural differences? What were those misunderstandings?
7. What were some of the highlights of your conversations?
8. What were your personal reactions to being around people from different cultures?
9. How would you do things differently next time you talked with this person or another person from the same cultural background?

Post Talk Journal Questions

1. What did you learn about how people from other cultures communicate and interact interpersonally?
2. What did you learn about yourself as an interpersonal communicator during intercultural interactions? What kinds of feelings arose for you as you talked with these people?
3. Describe one strength that you have as an intercultural communicator and one area for improvement.

Exercise 7.7: Metamessages and Intercultural Communication. This exercise is meant to be used with the articles by Begley and Chen & Starosta. Unless we tape record our conversations, it is almost impossible to hear how others hear us. We probably have more knowledge about the content of our speech than about our ways of speaking. It is possible to offend another person by the tone, volume, or even rate of our speech--and be oblivious to what we are communicating. While we traditionally think of conflicts between people as disagreements over ideology and perspective, conflicts can just as easily arise over how ideas are communicated. Such conflicts are based on the metamessages--messages about one's communication--people send when they use a certain tone or way of speaking to communicate. Metamessages provide a frame or context for understanding the messages we send (Stewart & D'Angelo, 1988). Metamessages during intercultural communication can be easily misunderstood because interactants do not have the same frame or context with which to interpret the communication.

This case study focuses on how conflicts can arise between culturally different people because of how metamessages are communicated. Have students read Carmina's story below. As they are reading, ask them to think about times when others have communicated with them in similar ways and situations when they have sent metamessages that might have been perceived as offensive or condescending, or were misinterpreted by people who are from different cultural or ethnic backgrounds.

Carmina works in an office with five other people. Ever since her supervisor hired her, Carmina has noticed that she talks much more slowly to her than to the native English speakers in the office. Carmina's first language is Spanish and she speaks flawless, accented English. Yet her supervisor still speaks to her using simple language at a markedly slow rate. No other person in the office speaks to Carmina in this way and two co-workers have even commented on the supervisor's annoying habit of speaking "special" English to her. It has become increasingly uncomfortable and offensive to talk with her but Carmina isn't sure how to bring up the subject. After all, she is new to the office and doesn't want to cause any problems--especially between her supervisor and her.

Questions for students to consider

1. Write down some reasons why the supervisor was using "special" English with Carmina. What was she thinking? What might have been her intentions?
2. Why might speaking in this way be offensive to people? When would it be appropriate?
3. How might Carmina go about talking with her supervisor about this issue?
4. How could Carmina's co-workers help?
5. As a non-native speaker of another language, have you ever faced the situation that Carmina is experiencing? Have you ever communicated with a non-native speaker the way Carmina's supervisor did with her? Describe what happened in either situation.
6. Describe a situation when someone sent metamessages that you found condescending or disrespectful. What happened and how did you handle the situation?
7. How can we let someone know that we find the way they are speaking to us offensive? Write down a few strategies.

Test Items for Chapter 7

<u>Multiple Choice</u>

1.   Which of the following is not a component of intercultural sensitivity?
     a.   judgment *
     b.   self-esteem
     c.   self-monitoring
     d.   interaction involvement

2.   Intercultural awareness refers to which of the following?
     a.   The cognitive aspect of intercultural communication.
     b.   Understanding cultural conventions and how they affect behavior.
     c.   Understanding cultural conventions and how they affect thought.
     d.   all of the above *

3.   Which of the following is an advantage of role-based training in groups?
     a.   it serves as a method of diagnosis
     b.   it provides opportunities for observing a variety of ways to deal with problems
     c.   it enables trainees to gain new insights that are important for cultural and self-understanding
     d.   all of the above *

4.   Individualistic conflict negotiators are more likely to attend to which of the following issues?
     a.   objective, substantive issues *
     b.   relational issues
     c.   socioemotional issues
     d.   issues of interpretation

5.   In collectivistic, high-context cultures, third party mediators are likely to be
     a.   impartial parties.
     b.   of lower status than the primary negotiators.
     c.   a professional mediator.
     d.   a person related to both parties of the dispute. *

6.   Which of the following statements is most accurate?
     a.   Individualistic cultures are more likely than collectivistic cultures to operate on M-time. *
     b.   Individualistic cultures are less likely than collectivistic cultures to operate on M-time.
     c.   Individualistic cultures are more likely than collectivistic cultures to operate on P-time.
     d.   There is no relationship between individualistic and collectivistic cultures and M- or P-time.

7. Individualistic, low-context cultures are more likely to value a conflict style that
   a. is indirect.
   b. uses the equality norm.
   c. uses the equity norm. *
   d. reflects the salience of a "we" identity.

8. Sauceda explains that the best pathway to improve mediation in a mental health context is at the
   a. clinical level
   b. psychotherapy level
   c. service delivery level
   d. education and training level *

9. Sauceda explains that if co-cultural folk medicine practices are weaved into this level then more rapport will be established with clients. The level he refers to is
   a. clinical level
   b. psychotherapy level *
   c. service delivery level
   d. education and training level

10. Which of the following is necessary to engage in a "mindfulness" state in intercultural interaction?
    a. being open to old information
    b. awareness of multiple perspectives *
    c. reinforcing existing categories
    d. thinking before speaking

11. Which one of the following is NOT one of the challenges of cross-cultural adaptation mentioned by Begley?
    a. ethnocentrism
    b. loneliness *
    c. disequalibrium
    d. level of knowledge

12. Experiencing emotional "lows" of uncertainty when one has crossed into another culture is identified by Begley as
    a. ethnocentrism
    b. cross-cultural depression
    c. disequilibrium *
    d. stagnation

13. Two words that capture the antithesis of ethnocentrism are:
     a.   kindness and patience
     b.   liberal and receptive
     c.   tolerant and progressive
     d.   openness and flexibility *

14. Which of the following is NOT one of the suggestions provided by Begley for successful cross-cultural adaptation?
     a.   frequency of time spent communicating
     b.   cultural background *
     c.   personal determination
     d.   personality characteristics

15. Which of the following approaches does Collier suggest for the study of culture?
     a.   culture as politics and ideology
     b.   culture as place
     c.   culture as performance
     d.   all of the above *

16. According to Collier, which of the following is the basis on which a group may define itself as a culture?
     a.   gender
     b.   geographical area
     c.   organization
     d.   all of the above *

17. Which of the following is a property or characteristic of cultural identities?
     a.   voluntary association with groups
     b.   involuntary association with groups
     c.   communication with others
     d.   all of the above *

18. Collier points out that the Peace Corps, once assumed to be a benevolent organization for the spread of resources to less developed parts of the world, is now often criticized for being a modern-day exporter of imperialism and colonialism. This shift in social perceptions might be studied using which of the following approaches to intercultural communication?
     a.   culture as ideology *
     b.   culture as psychology
     c.   culture as capital
     d.   culture as product

19. While *ascription* refers to how others view our identities ("This is who you are"), the process of *avowal* is best exemplified in which of the following statements?
    a. "This is who I think I am."
    b. "This is who I am to YOU."
    c. "This is who I am.." *
    d. 'This is who I think you think I am."

20. The term "feminisms" has been adopted by many feminists in an attempt to illustrate the _____ within that cultural identity.
    a. solidarity
    b. multivocality *
    c. universality
    d. none of the above

21. While a scholar aligned with the critical perspective might be concerned with the relationship between a particular cultural identity and its use and abuse of power, a scholar with a/an _____ perspective would be more interested in how the people who claim that cultural identity come to do, be, and know themselves as such.
    a. interactional
    b. interpretive *
    c. deconstructive
    d. empirical

True/False

T	1.	Intercultural awareness is the cognitive perspective of intercultural communication.
T	2.	Intercultural awareness requires individuals to understand that they are cultural beings.
T	3.	Intercultural awareness and sensitivity are the prerequisites for intercultural competence.
T	4.	Reciprocal determinism means that person variables, situation variables, and behavior continuously interact with one another.
T	5.	No one culture exists exclusively at one extreme of the communication context continuum.
F	6.	M-time cultures tend to view time as more contextually based and relationally oriented.
T	7.	Every intercultural conflict consists of both substantive and relational issues.
T	8.	The higher a person is in positional power in a collectivist culture, the more likely he or she will use silence as a deliberate, cautionary conflict strategy.
F	9.	Listening is synonymous with hearing.
T	10.	Avoiding conflict does not always mean that collectivists do not care about conflict.
F	11.	Admitting bias means perpetuating bias.

F	12.	One's personality is not a factor in whether or not one is able to successfully adapt to another culture.
F	13.	Language is usually not a major challenge in cross-cultural adaptation as long as the individual really wants to adapt.
T	14.	External factors influencing one's personal determination to successfully adapt to another culture include the length of stay in the host culture.
F	15.	Acquiring a broad base of knowledge about cultural differences is less effective for cross-cultural adaptation than to learn specific details about a culture one is about to visit.
T	16.	According to Collier, we become members of groups, in part, by learning about past members of the group.
F	17.	All groups of people who define themselves as a unit are cultures.
T	18.	Only when a group develops a history and hands down the symbols and norms to new members can it be said to have a cultural identity.
F	19.	The cognitive component of identity relates to the feelings we have about identity.
T	20.	Our identities emerge and develop as we interact with other people.

Essay Questions

1. Chen and Starosta claim that intercultural sensitivity enhances intercultural effectiveness. What do they mean by this? What would effectiveness include? Does it refer solely to overt success in the business world? To what else might it apply?

2. Define and explain the relationships between each of the following: intercultural awareness, sensitivity, and competence.

3. What do they mean when Chen and Starosta say that intercultural awareness necessitates that people understand themselves (not just others) as cultural beings? What are the implications of understanding oneself as a cultural being as opposed to a being that just appeared out of nowhere? What is the relationship between cultural awareness and a sense of history?

4. According to Baldwin and Hecht, identity is shared and developed only through communication. What are some ways that identity is shared in your culture? Provide examples of mediated and face-to-face ways you communicate your identity.

5. Using a specific identity; religious, ethnic, gender, sexual orientation, age cohort, social class, explain Baldwin and Hecht's three levels of identity.

6. How does Ting-Toomey define intercultural conflict?

7. Differentiate between "independent construal of self" and "interdependent construal of self".

8. Compare and contrast the value tendencies of individualism and collectivism.

9. What is the relationship between "in-groups" and "out-groups" and the individualism-collectivism dimension of value tendencies?

10. What is the relationship between low- and high-context cultures and cultures that are primarily individualistic or collectivistic with regard to approaches to conflict?

11. Describe the concept of "face" and its importance to understanding and engaging in intercultural conflict.

12. Identify three central issues for conflict in both individualistic, low-context cultures and collectivistic, high-context cultures.
13. Differentiate between the role of third party intervention in individualistic, low-context cultures and collectivistic, high-context cultures.
14. Describe the concept of "mindfulness" and its relevance to managing intercultural conflicts.
15. What does Sauceda mean when he suggests that we should employ "the freedom of silence" before using "the freedom of speech" as a way of being willing to be vulnerable and authentic?
16. Choose two of Begley's suggestions for successful cross-cultural adaptation and use your own cross-cultural experience to support them. Demonstrate how you applied these suggestions in a cross-cultural environment.
17. Using Begley's article, respond to the following statement: Learning a culture's language is only one step in the cross-cultural adaptation process.
18. Describe what Begley refers to as the *external* and *internal* factors involved in one's personal determination to successfully adapt to another culture.
19. Explain a communication perspective towards cultural identity.
20. Name and briefly describe three approaches to the study of culture outlined by Collier. Discuss Collier's understanding of the roles of power and ideology in the formation of cultural identities.
21. Define and give an example of Collier's Cultural Identity Types (CITs).
22. What might a communication perspective toward cultural identity take into consideration?
23. Define and discuss the relationship between avowal and ascription processes as discussed by Collier.

Chapter References

Brislin, R. W. (1994). Individualism and collectivism as the source of many specific cultural differences. In R. W. Brislin & T. Yoshida (Eds.), <u>Improving intercultural interactions: Modules for cross-cultural training</u>. London: Sage Publications.

Stewart, J., & D'Angelo, G. (1988). <u>Together: Communication interpersonally</u> (3rd ed.). New York: Random House.

Chapter 8
Ethical Considerations: Prospects for the Future

Chapter Synopsis

This chapter explores the issue of ethics and intercultural communication. The five articles in this chapter touch on ethical and philosophical considerations when members of diverse cultures must live together. In short, this chapter offers various perspectives on developing and improving intercultural communication so that diverse cultures can live together without destroying each other.

In the chapter's first article, Cleveland introduces students to the ethics and philosophical assumptions surrounding intercultural communication. Instead of fear and tribal loyalties, he advocates "civilization" as universal values, ideas, and practices that are accepted as useful everywhere in order to form a global civil society. Kim proposes that becoming intercultural persons with intercultural personhood is essential in order for different cultures and countries to get along. Shuter's essay examines the ethnocentrism of current literature on communication ethics, and discusses the challenges Confucianist and Hindu ethical systems present to this literature. He asks the important question: "Can a communication ethics emerge that transcends culture and serves as a guideline when communicating interculturally?" (452). Nussbaum shows us another view toward an intercultural ethic by examining how people must operate as citizens of the world with sensitivity and understanding. Nussbaum's article provides students with a historical overview of some well-known philosophers. Finally, Kale's article proposes that we use the human spirit as an organizing concept for a universal value system. People of all cultures, Kale claims, have in common a human spirit that gives them the ability to make value decisions and attempt to live a fulfilling life.

Discussion Ideas

1. Explain Cleveland's concept of civilization, Are universal laws and rules possible? Why or why not?

2. How do we adopt Kim's notion of intercultural personhood? What characteristics do we include in this concept? Which do we exclude?

3. What does Shuter mean when he states that communication ethicists need to admit the intracultural bias of their research? What does he mean by suggesting communicators journey *intraculturally*?

4. Explain what it means to be a citizen of the world? How can one maintain their sense of culture while being a citizen of the world?

5. "Therefore, the guiding principle of any universal code of intercultural communication should be to protect the worth and dignity of the human spirit." What cultural assumptions and values does Kale use in proposing the human spirit as the organizing concept of a universal code of ethics? Freedom? Equality? Spirituality?

6. What do you think of Kale's four principles that make up his universal code of ethics? Are these enough? Do you agree? What are they lacking? Principle #1 sounds like the golden rule, but how about the platinum rule: Do unto others as they would have you do unto them? Respect them the way they wish to be respected, not the way you would like to be respected. Would this be a more appropriate rule for intercultural interactions since not all cultures show respect in the same way, for the same reasons, to the same people, etc.?

Exercises

Exercise 8.1: Cultural Universals. This activity can be used with Cleveland's article on cultural diversity and asks the students to think seriously about the growing diversity in the United States as well as the idea of "wholeness incorporating diversity." Divide students into small groups and have them reread the following excerpt from Cleveland's article:

> ... *civilization* is what's universal -- values, ideas, and practices that are in general currency everywhere, either because they are viewed as objectively "true" or because they are accepted pragmatically as useful in the existing circumstances. These accepted "truths" offer the promise of weaving together a *civitas* of universal laws and rules, becoming the basis for a global civil society. (p. 434)

After reading the excerpt, have students make a list of laws, rules, or practices that are generally accepted on a universal basis. (Cleveland offers, as one example, the international exchange of money). Groups must be prepared to defend the universality of these items. Additionally, have the groups create a list of laws, rules, and practices that they believe would contribute to pluralism if they were universal. Again, groups must support and defend their answers. When the groups have completed their lists, write on the board those laws, rules, and practices that were common among all groups. Have the students discuss the reality of these ideas being enacted and their effect on individual communities, the US, and the world.

Exercise 8.2: The East-West Game. This activity is an accompaniment for Kim's article on intercultural personhood or combining key attributes of the East and West. The East-West Game was originally entitled "The Emperor's Pot" and first developed by Donald Batchelder of the Experiment in International Living (Hoopes & Ventura, 1979). It simulates a negotiation session between two very different cultures. By taking part in this intercultural negotiation session, students will be able to test their ability to communicate with a culture that thinks and behaves in very different ways. The problems that often occur during intercultural communication will also be illustrated.

This activity is most useful when conducted over two or three class sessions. The exercise has been adapted to accommodate the university classroom and allow all participants to either watch or take part in the entire process. There are four phases in the activity: Phase I --

students are divided into two groups and given time to "adopt" their new culture and plan their negotiation session. Phase II --class regroups and the negotiations begin. Phase III --East and West meet in their own groups to discuss what happened. Phase IV--class discussion. (Phase III can be left out if there is a time constraint.)

The negotiations center on a highly coveted cultural artifact that the East has and the West wants. The West has come to the East to negotiate for the artifact. The handouts on the next two pages provide each team with instructions for the activity.

Questions to stimulate discussion during the debriefing afterward:

1. What cultural traits characterized your culture?
2. What traits did you notice in the other culture?
3. How difficult was it to put on another culture?
4. How did your own individual and cultural traits prevent you from fully adopting the East or West culture?
5. How did you plan your approach to the negotiations?
6. Did you attempt to determine how the other side might behave?
7. Were your assumptions correct?
8. Did you notice any differences in nonverbal behavior between the two groups? The use of verbal language?
9. During the negotiations, when did you first notice that there might be a problem?
10. What barriers caused this problem?
11. Was this barrier broken and productive negotiations allowed to continue?
12. What strategies were used to be culturally sensitive?
13. What strategies were used to get the artifact or keep it from the other team?
14. How could the negotiations have been more successful?

Exercise 8.2: The East-West Game (Hoopes & Ventura, 1979)

Instructions for the East

Your group represents an ancient Eastern culture that although poor, is very proud of its long history and heritage. You have a highly treasured artifact that is as old as 400 AD. It is *the* national treasure and culturally you cannot give it up. The West wants this artifact and has been strongly pressured to return with it. (You may wish to identify a single behavior demonstrated by the West that will win them the artifact.)

What complicates these negotiations is that you come from a culture that is very agreeable, polite, and always seeking to answer in the affirmative whether you mean "yes" or not. You never state anything as flatly negative during negotiation sessions. You never tell your opposing team that they will never get the artifact. Sometimes you may stop the negotiations to talk amongst yourselves. You always seem to agree and go along with the other team because offending another party might result in the other losing face,

You do not use strong, direct eye contact. You occasionally look them in the eye but never for prolonged periods of time nor with any degree of intensity. Using mediation is common in your culture. For example, although the Chief Spokesman may do a lot of the talking he will very often ask his- team members what they think. He will often allow other members to speak and carry on the negotiations with the other side.

Before meeting the other team, look at the following list of roles and cultural traits. Decide who will have each role, adopt the cultural traits that govern your culture, and choose an approach you will take in the negotiations.

Roles

Chief Spokesman, Minister of Education and Culture, Security Officer, Political Officer, Protocol Officer, Information Officer, Recorder (to list all the assumptions, values, etc., of other side), Time-keeper (to keep each phase exactly on schedule), GOD (Group Organizational Director) -the overall organizer of the East Team, Most Honored Grandmother, Spokesman (most honored), Advisors --- all others.

Cultural Traits

"We": the group is most highly valued, not the individual. Individual always in social role. Cannot do anything to conflict with group.
Form: Outward form is most important. Manners extremely important, must participate in activities considered important by group, even if one disagrees.
Nature: Conformity to the rules of nature is best.
Progress: Change is both negative and positive. Technical change necessary, social change bad.
Efficiency: Considered less important than higher values such as form, saving face, conformity to custom.
Time: Not precisely measured, not primary consideration. Present, not future, given priority.
Humility: Related to one's social status. One never takes advantage of one's rank. One must always defer to one of higher social rank, must always try to appear humble.
Money: Saving for the sake of saving is seldom considered a virtue. Price is regarded as an index of quality.
Age: Great reverence for age. Age means wisdom and certain privileges. Honorific titles are always used when addressing an elder. Person of higher rank must attempt to defer to and honor special inferiors.
Education: Highly valued. Means of raising whole family status.
Authority: Obedience to authority, individual rights mean little.
Moral Superiority: A moral smugness that stems from a conviction that East people are a special people with a set of values and conditions that make them unique.

Exercise 8.2: The East-West Game (Hoopes & Ventura, 1979)

Instructions for the West

Your group represents a Western culture that is rich and powerful. There is a highly treasured artifact in the possession of the East that is a highly valued part of their heritage. They are a poor country but will be very reluctant to give up the artifact. Your national museum and your government have strongly urged you to get the artifact at any cost. Money is no problem. You cannot come out and say that you will get the artifact at any cost because the East is world renowned as shrewd traders. But you believe that every person has his/her price.

Culturally, you feel it is important to try to figure out the strategies acceptable to the other side so that you can enter and progress through the negotiations smoothly. But you should always try to stay within the cultural traits listed below. You are success-oriented, hard-working, efficient, future-oriented, and you use time productively. You like to move things along.

Before meeting the other team, look at the following list of roles and cultural traits. Decide who will have each role, adopt the cultural traits that govern your culture, and choose an approach you will take in the negotiations.

Roles

Curator of National Museum (expert on Oriental Art); Millionaire (major donor of museum); Diplomatic Officer; Public Relations man or woman; CIA agent posing as an Area Studies Specialist; Journalist; Chief of your task-group (forceful administrator); Recorder -- to list all assumptions, values, etc., of other side; Time-keeper -- to keep each phase of exercise exactly on schedule; GOD (Group Organizational Director) -- the overall organizer of the West team; Advisors -- all others

Cultural Traits

"I": ego-centric.
Individualism: self-reliance and initiative expected from other side. Status achieved from own efforts. Achievement is good and requires competitiveness. Competition is expected.
Social Conformity: Outward conformity to opinions of others has certain value.
Activism: Being active and "on top of things," especially when uncertain, is a virtue. Achievement and goal-oriented activities stressed.
Pragmatism: Practical ingenuity applied to social and materialistic problems.
Progress: Change in itself is good. Humans must work to control nature.
Efficiency: Social organizations and individuals must be efficient.
Time: Precisely measured and must be used productively and efficiently.
Aggressiveness: Ambition, competition, and self-assertiveness to achieve success are emphasized.
Money: An economic tool and yardstick for social status, influence, power, satisfaction.
Youth: Highly valued. Old people wish they were young again.
Education: Means to an end. Reflection on family prestige. Means to attain skill, money, status.
Authority: Rules/laws generally obeyed, but don't like to be ordered to obey. Authority must not infringe on individual rights.
Moral Superiority: A moral smugness that stems from a conviction that West people are a special people with a set of values and conditions that make them unique.

Exercise 8.3: Are We Really Citizens of the World? This activity asks students to consider those behaviors which they find acceptable and those which they find unacceptable and what they base those beliefs on. It is designed to be used in conjunction with Nussbaum's article. Nussbaum's article states that:

> As readers of the *Life of Diogenes*, we quickly become aware of the cultural relativity of what is thought shocking. For one of the most shocking things about Diogenes, to his Athenian contemporaries, was his habit of eating in the public marketplace. It was this habit that gave him the name "dog", *kuon*, from which our English label Cynic derives. Only dogs, in this culture, tore away at their food in full view of all. Athenians evidently found this just about as outrageous as public masturbation; in fact his biographer joins the two offenses together saying, "He used to do everything in public both the deeds of Demeter and those of Aphrodite. (p. 460)

With this in mind, have students generate their own list of those behaviors which they find to be "shocking" or unacceptable in their culture and those that are acceptable. Have students then meet in small groups with other students in the class to discuss the differences and similarities on their lists. What do most find to be acceptable behavior? Unacceptable behavior? Are their any surprises that arise from this discussion?

This discussion allows students an opportunity to express their beliefs, listen to the beliefs of others, learn to understand why some behaviors are considered acceptable in some cultures while yet unacceptable in others. Most importantly in the discussion is the concept of being "Citizens of the World" which invites students to become aware of others beliefs and behaviors and seeing them from the vantage point of the outsider in order to inquire about their meaning and function of these beliefs.

Exercise 8.4: Universal Ethics in Intercultural Communication. This activity takes students out of the classroom and is designed to be used in conjunction with Kale's article on peace as an ethic for intercultural communication. Kale states that:

> The concept of peace applies not only to relations between cultures and countries, but also to the right of all people to live at peace with themselves and their surroundings. As such it is unethical to communicate with people in a way that violates their concept of themselves or the dignity and worth of their human spirit. (p. 469)

With this notion in mind, have students examine recent media events to find two examples. First, have them find a media example in which this notion was NOT adhered to. Was minimal, moderate, or optimal peace the result? Compare and contrast the results if the situation were hypothetically reversed and Kale's concept of peace were applied. What level of peace could be anticipated? Second, have the students find a recent media event in which some or all of Kale's four principles for a universal code of ethics were applied. Identify the principles and the outcome of the situation. What level of peace was achieved? What might have been the result if these principles were not applied? Have students discuss their findings with the class.

Exercise 8.5: What If . . . . We know that how we react to people is based on how we perceive them and their actions. Our world is based on our perceptions of others and their perceptions of us. Oftentimes, these perceptions are not based on personal information about others as individuals but on cultural information gleaned from the media, family, and friends. That is, we use previously gathered information from a variety of sources to perceive and understand new people that we meet.

Ask students to imagine developing a relationship (platonic or romantic) with individuals who hold each given perception of the world below. This exercise can be conducted in small groups or as an individual in or out-of-class assignment. Some questions to ask students during a large class discussion are: How might a certain belief affect your relationship with this imaginary person? Does your perception of the world fit or complement your friend's or partner's? Or are your perceptions diametrically at odds? How can we communicate and develop intercultural relationships when our world views can oftentimes be so different? What must we consider as you attempt to communicate with people who do not share your world view?

HOW MIGHT YOUR RELATIONSHIP BE AFFECTED IF . . .

1. . . . your spouse believed in reincarnation and karma?
2. . . . your friend believed that all events in the world are determined by Fate?
3. . . . your friend believed that certain ethnic or racial groups are intellectually inferior?
4. . . . your significant other believed that women are superior to men? that men were superior to women?
5. . . . your roommates believed that the rights of groups are more important than those of the individual.? the rights of the individual are more important than those of the group?
6. . . . a new friend believed adamantly that homosexuality is immoral and should not be accepted by society as normal.? that homosexuality is moral and should be accepted?
7. . . . your neighbor believed in using only traditional medicine and spiritual healing whenever she or her family became ill?

Exercise 8.6: "Mom and Dad, Guess What....?". Students may experience or have experienced forming an intimate relationship with someone of whom their family and friends disapproved, or may have a friend or relative who has had this experience. Such situations often occur because our family and friends have certain expectations about who are appropriate dating and marriage partners. These expectations are firmly entrenched in our perceptions of people who are different from us and in cultural norms of relationship development and sexual behavior. Our families can have a profound impact on the development and success of our romantic relationships.

The following exercise asks students to imagine that they have developed certain relationships of which their parents may not approve and that they are coming home to talk with them about their decision. The goal of this exercise is threefold. First, it will allow students to consider how their parents might react to the news that they are about to marry someone of a different political belief, religion, or ethnicity, or of the same sex. In addition this exercise will allow them to think about how they might react as a parent to their own child's news of marriage. Finally, we have designed this exercise to offer valuable insight into how attitudes toward nontraditional marriages have changed in the past three decades.

Ask students to roleplay with another classmate the following scenes. They are to take on the role of their parents and the role of themselves as parents.

Your Parents

> Think about your parents' attitudes about marriage, relationships , and cultural differences. How would they react if you told them you were going to marry someone who:
>
> 1.   had a disability?
> 2.   was of a different religion?
> 3.   was of a different ethnicity?
> 4.   was of the same sex?
>
> We realize that you cannot truly know how your parents would react (unless you have seen their reactions to one or more of these situations) but try to imagine how they would respond given your understanding of who they are and their belief systems.

You as a Parent

> Now take on the role of the parent. How would you react if your child told you he or she was going to marry someone . . . .
>
> 1.   who had a disability? Why would you react this way?
> 2.   was of a different religion? Why would you react this way?
> 3.   was of a different ethnicity? Why would you react this way?
> 4.   was of the same sex? Why would you react this way?
>
> We realize that unless you are a parent, you probably do not know how you would react to your child given these circumstances. Again, try to imagine given your present belief and value systems.

Analysis of Your Responses

> 1.   What differences do you see between your responses and what you believe would be your parents' responses?
> 2.   What is acceptable today that was not in the 1950s and 1960s? What attitudes have largely not changed very much at all?

3.   How might a family be affected by nontraditional and intercultural marriages?
4.   Have you or a member of your family ever entered into a marriage with someone who was culturally different or different from what was "expected"? If so, describe how people reacted to this new family member.

Test Items for Chapter 8

Multiple Choice

1.   What factor does Cleveland identify as a primary incentive for people to develop multiple personalities with plural group loyalties?
   a.   This is a more mobile world as evidenced by the fact that in 1994 more people moved than ever before in world history. *
   b.   Fear has caused people to become loyal to only one group.
   c.   Political structures are being questioned.
   d.   None of the above.

2.   According to Cleveland, two major impediments to better standards of life and freedom for all are
   a.   technology and class differences.
   b.   human rights and poverty.
   c.   culture and diversity. *
   d.   diversity and human rights.

3.   According to Cleveland, in the East, a concept is understood through _____ is one of complete meaning and immediately experienced, apprehended, and contemplated.
   a.   analysis
   b.   emotion
   c.   spiritualism
   d.   intuition *

4.   What does the term "undifferentiated" mean in terms of Eastern philosophy and consciousness?
   a.   wholeness *
   b.   uniqueness
   c.   distinctness
   d.   serenity

5.   The relationship of the views of East and West can best be described as
   a.   competing
   b.   antagonistic
   c.   complementary *
   d.   dualistic

6.   Western thought tends to equate logic with
      a.   necessity
      b.   truth *
      c.   progress
      d.   correctness

7.   Which of the following does Johannesen NOT give as a defining characteristic of an
      ethical issue in communication?
      a.   Voluntarily choosing a communication strategy
      b.   The communication strategy is based on a value judgment
      c.   When two interactants are of unequal status *
      d.   The chosen strategy could affect someone else

8.   According to Shuter, which of the following is true of Shintoism?
      a.   It has no concept of good and evil *
      b.   It invests only humans with spirits
      c.   It considers reason integral to ethical choices
      d.   All of the above

9.   Communicator ethics in Confucian philosophy is based on which of the following?
      a.   obligation to family to the exclusion of society at large
      b.   reverence for elders *
      c.   greater concern for society at large than for family
      d.   a & b

10.   Which of the following are considered paths to enlightenment in Hindu thought?
      a.   emotion *
      b.   reason
      c.   pragmatic connections
      d.   a & c

11.   Who called freedom of speech the finest thing in human life?
      a.   Plato
      b.   Diogenes *
      c.   Socrates
      d.   Aristotle

12.   Whose habit of eating in the public marketplace gave him the name of "dog"?
      a.   Plato
      b.   Diogenes *
      c.   Socrates
      d.   Aristotle

13. Who claimed, "I am a Citizen of the World'?
    a.   Plato
    b.   Diogenes *
    c.   Socrates
    d.   Aristotle

14. Stoic thought was a major formative influence on which of the following?
    a.   Emerson
    b.   Thoreau
    c.   both a and b *
    d.   none of the above

15. On what concept does Kale base his universal code of ethics?
    a.   human spirit *
    b.   human dignity
    c.   humaneness
    d.   human volition

True/False

T   1.   According to Cleveland, the "civilization" construct will work because nobody is in charge of practices that are generally accepted.
F   2.   Traditions of separateness and discrimination are always permanent and immutable.
F   3.   In earlier times, the waves of new Americans learned to tolerate each other as individuals and then as groups.
T   4   According to Kim, the Western view of the world is characteristically dualistic, materialistic, and lifeless.
T   5.   In the East, a virtuous person is not one who only strives for the "good" and eliminates the "bad" but one who strives for a balance between the two.
F   6.   The Western perception of time is best represented as a wheel that is continually turning.
F   7.   Explicit and clear verbalization best characterizes the Eastern way of communicating.
T   8.   The West is concerned more than the East with building greater ego strength.
T   9.   In Islamic ethics, intellectualism for its own sake is "a sin against human nature—maybe even a crime."
F   10.   Confucian thought elevates reason and logic to the sublime.
T   11.   Ethical messages within Hindu thought should in some way move people closer to liberation.
F   12.   Morals are the basis for communication ethics.
T   13.   There is no such thing as a totally individual system of ethics.
F   14.   Moderate peace refers to the absence of conflict.
T   15.   U.S. and Canada may be said to maintain an optimal peace.

T   16.   All religions harbor images of peace constructed in "sacred places."
T   17.   In Plato's Republic the plan for the ideal city is plainly influenced by reflection about customs elsewhere.
T   18.   Diogenes disdained external markers of status and focused on the inner life of virtue and thought.

Essay Questions

1.   Identify some of the reasons Cleveland believes the U.S. is moving toward pluralism.
2.   How do Eastern and Western peoples view the relationship of nature and humans?
3.   What is the differentiated aesthetic continuum?
4.   How do Western and Eastern peoples traditionally conceptualize knowledge?
5.   How do the East and West perceive time differently?
6.   How do Eastern and Western views of relationships, groups, and the self differ?
7.   How does one communicate one's feelings in Eastern and Western culture.
8.   Describe how our lives demand both scientific and aesthetic modes of apprehension.
9.   What are the benefits of incorporating an Eastern aesthetic orientation into Western life?
10.   How would you explain the connection between reflexivity about one's own culture and intercultural communication? Does Shuter model reflexivity about his culture in his writing? If yes, explain how.
11.   How do Western notions of communication ethics reflect a Judeo-Christian perspective?
12.   What is "intercultural personhood" and how and why should we strive to attain it?
13.   What is the basic premise of cultural relativity?
14.   What does it mean to be a citizen of the world?
15.   Explain why people could perceive some of Diogenes' behavior as shocking while other behaviors of his were not viewed as being such?
16.   Describe Kale's notion of the human spirit as an organizing concept on which to base a universal code of ethics.
17.   Describe the three different kinds of peace mentioned by Kale.
18.   On what four principles does Kale base his code of universal ethics?

Chapter References

Hoopes, D. S., & Ventura, P. (Eds.). (1979). Intercultural sourcebook: Cross-cultural training methodologies. LaGrange Park, IL: Intercultural Network.